Reflections

California:
A CHANGING STATE

Homework and
Practice Book

Grade 4

D1530904

Harcourt
SCHOOL PUBLISHERS

Orlando   Austin   New York   San Diego   Toronto   London

Visit *The Learning Site!*
www.harcourtschool.com

Photo Credits

99 CORBIS

Printed in the United States of America

ISBN 0-15-341479-0

15 16 17   1413   14 13 12 1 10 09

Reflections

The activities in this book reinforce social studies concepts and skills in Harcourt School Publisher's *Reflections: California: A Changing State*. There is one activity for each lesson and skill. In addition to activities, this book also contains reproductions of the Reading Social Studies graphic organizers that appear in the chapter reviews in the Student Edition. Study guides for student reviews are also provided. Reproductions of the activities pages appear with answers in the Teacher Edition.

Contents

UNIT 1: THE LAND AND EARLY PEOPLE

UNIT 2: EARLY CALIFORNIA

UNIT 3: THE ROAD TO STATEHOOD

UNIT 4: GROWTH AND DEVELOPMENT

UNIT 5: PROGRESS AS A STATE

UNIT 6: CALIFORNIA TODAY AND TOMORROW

Name _____ Date _____

California's Location

DIRECTIONS For each sentence, circle the word or phrase that makes it correct.

1. The equator divides Earth into
   the Northern Hemisphere and the Southern Hemisphere /
   the Western Hemisphere and the Eastern Hemisphere.

2. California is in the Northern Hemisphere / Southern Hemisphere.

3. The prime meridian divides Earth into
   the Northern Hemisphere and the Southern Hemisphere /
   the Western Hemisphere and the Eastern Hemisphere.

4. California is in the Western Hemisphere / Eastern Hemisphere.

5. California is located on the continent of Europe / North America.

6. California is part of the Hawaiian Islands / the Pacific Basin.

7. California is in the country of Canada / the United States of America.

8. California is in the region of our country known as the South / the West.

9. California is an Atlantic Coast state / a Pacific Coast state.

10. California is east / west of the ocean that borders it.

11. California is north / south of Mexico.

12. The Colorado River forms part of California's eastern / western border.

13. California is east / west of Arizona.

14. California is east / west of Nevada.

15. California is north / south of Oregon.

CALIFORNIA STANDARDS HSS 4.1, 4.1.2

Skills: Use Latitude and Longitude

DIRECTIONS Jeanine wrote a letter to her best friend, Luisa. Since they both like detective stories, she decided to write her message in code. Jeanine used latitude and longitude to tell about her trip. Study the map on page 3, and read Jeanine's letter below. Identify the place near each of the lines of latitude and longitude in Jeanine's message. Write the name of the place in the blank.

Dear Luisa,

I know how much you like being a "detective"! Use a map, and see if you can figure out where my family and I went on our trip!

As you know, we started out from a city near 34°N, 118°W,

_____—no mystery there! We stayed close to home the

first night—in a city near 35°N, 119°W, _____,
with my cousins. The next day, we drove to a city near 37°N, 120°W,

_____, to have lunch with my mom's friend. Then we

went on to a national park near 38°N, 119°W, _____.
That is an awesome place!

From there, it was on to the city near 38°N, 122°W,

_____. We spent two days sightseeing there. Then we

took the long trip to see a place near 41°N, 122°W, _____.
You might say that was the "high point" of our vacation!

When we started back home, we stopped for a day in a city near 39°N, 122°W,

_____. Then we got up early and drove to a place

near 36°N, 117°W, _____. Even though this was
the "low point" of our trip, it was still a hot spot! From there, we went to

_____, a national park near 36°N, 119°W. I was
there once before and I still really like it. On our last day, we drove past

_____, near 35°N, 118°W, and finally came home.
What a great state I live in!

Your friend,

Jeanine

CALIFORNIA STANDARDS HSS 4.1, 4.1.1, 4.1.2; CS 4 *(continued)*

© Harcourt

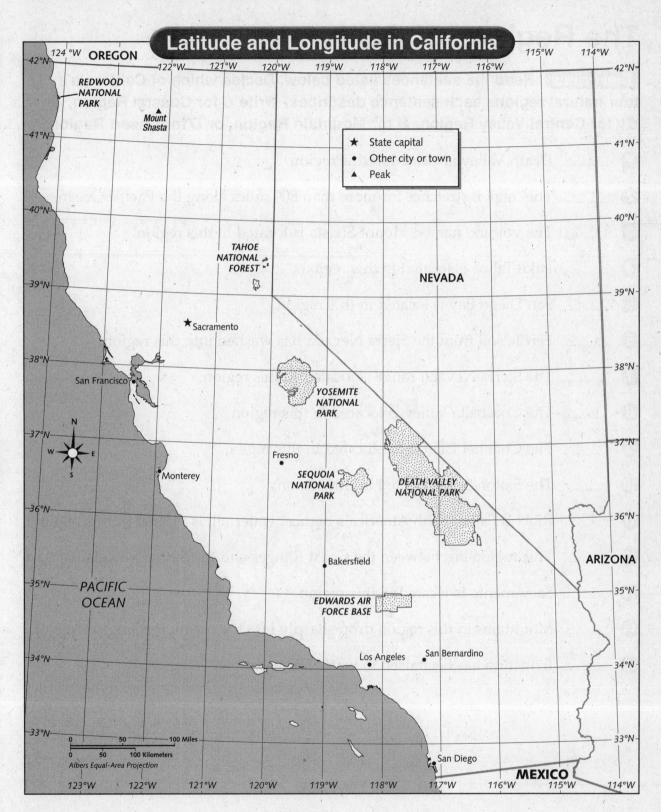

Latitude and Longitude in California

OREGON 124°W · 122°W · 121°W · 120°W · 119°W · 118°W · 117°W · 116°W · 115°W · 114°W

REDWOOD NATIONAL PARK

▲ Mount Shasta

★ State capital
● Other city or town
▲ Peak

TAHOE NATIONAL FOREST

NEVADA

★ Sacramento

San Francisco ●

YOSEMITE NATIONAL PARK

Fresno ●

Monterey ●

SEQUOIA NATIONAL PARK

DEATH VALLEY NATIONAL PARK

PACIFIC OCEAN

Bakersfield ●

ARIZONA

EDWARDS AIR FORCE BASE

Los Angeles ● San Bernardino ●

San Diego ●

MEXICO

0 50 100 Miles
0 50 100 Kilometers
Albers Equal-Area Projection

123°W · 122°W · 121°W · 120°W · 119°W · 118°W · 117°W · 116°W · 115°W · 114°W

© Harcourt

Name _____ Date _____

The Regions of California

DIRECTIONS Read the sentences listed below. Decide which of California's four natural regions each sentence describes. Write *C* for Coastal Region, *CV* for Central Valley Region, *M* for Mountain Region, or *D* for Desert Region.

1 _____ Death Valley is located in this region.

2 _____ This region stretches for more than 800 miles along the Pacific Ocean.

3 _____ The volcano named Mount Shasta is located in this region.

4 _____ Lake Tahoe is located in this region.

5 _____ San Diego Bay is located in this region.

6 _____ Fertile soil from the Sierra Nevada has washed into this region.

7 _____ The Sierra Nevada range is located in this region.

8 _____ The Coachella Valley is located in this region.

9 _____ The Channel Islands are located in this region.

10 _____ The Salton Sea is located in this region.

11 _____ Ribbon Falls, North America's highest waterfall, is located in this region.

12 _____ This region lies between the Coast Ranges and the Sierra Nevada.

13 _____ Sacramento is located in this region.

14 _____ Mountains in this region drop sharply into the ocean, forming steep cliffs.

15 _____ Irrigation has been used to water farmland in this region.

CALIFORNIA STANDARDS HSS 4.1, 4.1.3, 4.1.4; HI 2

Name _____ Date _____

Skills: Use an Elevation Map

DIRECTIONS Study the elevation map of Yosemite National Park below. Then use the map to decide what is the correct elevation for each location. Circle the correct answer.

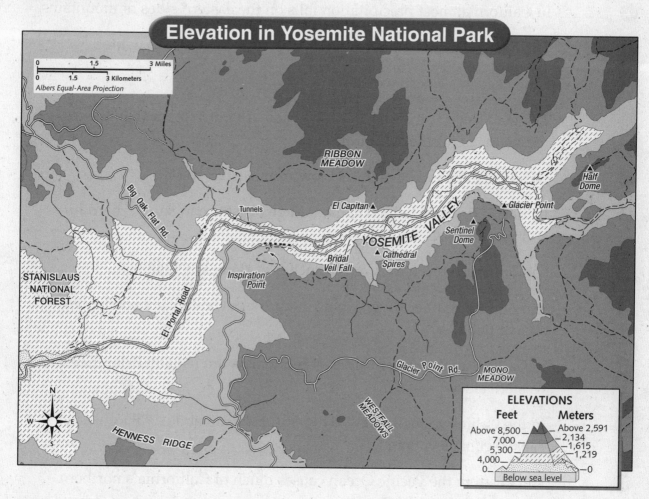

1	**Inspiration Point**	3,391 ft	5,391 ft	7,391 ft
2	**Bridal Veil Fall**	4,787 ft	6,787 ft	8,787 ft
3	**Cathedral Spires**	4,114 ft	6,114 ft	8,114 ft
4	**Sentinel Dome**	4,117 ft	6,117 ft	8,117 ft
5	**El Capitan**	5,042 ft	7,042 ft	9,042 ft

© Harcourt

CALIFORNIA STANDARDS HSS 4.1, 4.1.3, 4.1.4; CS 4

Climate and Vegetation

DIRECTIONS Read each sentence about California's climate and vegetation. Decide whether each statement is true (*T*) or false (*F*).

1 _____ In California, most precipitation falls on the eastern sides of mountains.

2 _____ The Pacific Ocean helps warm the land near the coast in winter.

3 _____ San Diego has a very wet climate.

4 _____ The giant sequoias of the Sierra Nevada are much taller than the redwoods of northern California.

5 _____ Winds in California generally blow from east to west.

6 _____ In 2003, a drought helped cause a huge brushfire in San Bernardino and San Diego Counties.

7 _____ San Francisco receives about 80 inches of rain each year.

8 _____ In 1997, the Feather River Valley in northern California experienced a great flood.

9 _____ In California, the eastern sides of mountains are usually drier than the western sides.

10 _____ In the California mountains, temperatures drop about 3°F for every 1,000 feet of elevation.

11 _____ Wet air from the Pacific Ocean causes much of California's northern coast to be rainy and foggy.

12 _____ The Sierra Nevada receives small amounts of snow in the winter.

13 _____ Some California redwoods grow taller than 350 feet.

14 _____ Deserts often form in a rain shadow.

15 _____ Great amounts of rainfall help giant trees, such as the coast redwoods, grow in northern California.

© Harcourt

CALIFORNIA STANDARDS HSS 4.1, 4.1.3; HI 2

Where Californians Live

DIRECTIONS Read the information below about Los Angeles. Pretend you are writing a real estate brochure and that you want people to move to the city. Write a paragraph to try to persuade people to move there. Use whatever facts you think are necessary to write your paragraph.

- Approximately 3,864,000 people live in the city of Los Angeles. The largest group is in the 25- to 29-year-old age range.

- In 1997, there were 255 libraries in Los Angeles with a total of 19,714,733 books.

- The average daily high/low temperature ranged from 83°F/63°F in August to 66°F/47°F in January.

- In a recent school year, the average class size in Los Angeles County was 27 students.

- In 2000, about 4 out of every 10 Californians spoke a language other than English at home.

- Los Angeles County has 30 miles of beaches and about 20 public beaches.

_____

_____

_____

_____

_____

© Harcourt

CALIFORNIA STANDARDS HSS 4.1, 4.1.3, 4.1.4; HI 2

skills: Read a Population Map

DIRECTIONS Look at the population map below. Use the map to compare the populations of cities in California. For Items 1 through 5, circle which city has the higher population density. For Items 6 through 10, circle which city has the lower population density.

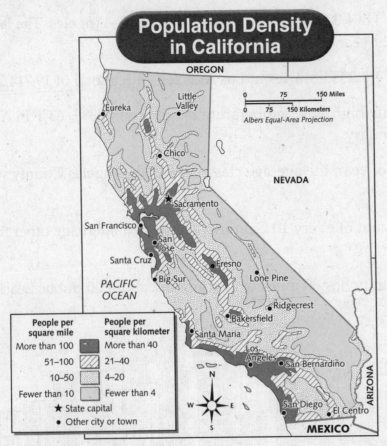

Population Density in California

Which has a higher population density?	Which has a lower population density?
1 Ridgecrest San Jose	**6** Chico Little Valley
2 El Centro San Bernardino	**7** Big Sur Santa Cruz
3 San Jose Santa Maria	**8** Bakersfield San Diego
4 Chico Lone Pine	**9** Eureka Lone Pine
5 El Centro Fresno	**10** Ridgecrest Sacramento

 CALIFORNIA STANDARDS HSS 4.1, 4.1.5; CS 4

© Harcourt

Life in California

DIRECTIONS Fill in the chart below about life in the regions of California. Write a brief description for each factor in column 2.

Region	Factors Affecting Life in this Region
Coastal Region	**1** Important industries: Fishing and timber are important industries. **2** Earthquakes: _____
Central Valley	**3** Fertile soil: _____ _____ **4** Important crops: _____ _____
Mountain Region	**5** Popular sports: _____ _____ **6** Natural resources: _____ _____
Desert Region	**7** Irrigation: _____ **8** Natural resources: _____ _____

© Harcourt

CALIFORNIA STANDARDS HSS 4.1, 4.1.3; HI 2

Name _____ Date _____

Study Guide

DIRECTIONS Fill in the missing words in this school radio announcement for California. Use the terms below to help you complete the announcement for each lesson. You will have to use some words twice.

Lesson 1	Lesson 2	Lesson 3	Lesson 4	Lesson 5
Hemisphere	harbors	precipitation	urban	service
equator	fertile	climates	metropolitan	industry
prime	sea level	humid	areas	faults
meridian	coastal plain	rain shadow	suburbs	growing
relative	irrigation	drought	rural	season
location			modify	

Lesson 1   California is a great place to live! It has a convenient

_____, bordering the Pacific Ocean. California is located

north of the_____ in the Northern _____,

and west of the _____ in the Western _____.

Lesson 2   Along California's shoreline is a low-lying _____

and two large natural _____, where ships can dock safely.

California's Central Valley has _____ soil, making it great for

growing crops. In the dry deserts, people have used _____

to water their farmland. California even has the lowest spot in the

Western Hemisphere—Death Valley, which is an amazing 282 feet below

_____!

CALIFORNIA STANDARDS HSS 4.1, 4.1.2, 4.1.3, 4.1.4

(continued)

10 ■ **Homework and Practice Book**   Use after reading Chapter 1, pages 12–47.

© Harcourt

Name _____ Date _____

Lesson 3   Weather in California is exciting. Too much rain, and you get a flood. Too little, and you get a _____. Even nearby areas can have different _____. Do you like the mountains? Well, they can block in moist, or _____, air. The west sides of mountains have a lot of rainfall, or _____. The east sides are drier. They lie in an area called the _____. Deserts can form here.

Lesson 4   There are many different places in California where people live. Some people live in cities, or _____ areas. These cities, together with their smaller, nearby _____, make up large _____. Other people prefer living in _____ areas—home to forests, farms, and ranches. Californians have even started moving into desert areas now that they have learned to _____ their environment.

Lesson 5   So where in California will you go? And in what field, or _____, will you choose to work? Will you provide a _____ to others, such as being a firefighter or a police officer? Maybe you will live in the Coastal Region and be an engineer. You could help design safer buildings in areas that are located near _____. Would you like to live in the Central Valley Region? There are a lot of jobs there in the farming _____, due to the long _____ there. No matter what you decide, you'll find a place for yourself in California!

© Harcourt

Name _____ Date _____

READING SOCIAL STUDIES: MAIN IDEA AND DETAILS

⭐ Focus Skill California's Geography

DIRECTIONS Complete the graphic organizer to show that you understand important ideas and details about California's natural regions.

Main Idea

California's natural regions have different physical and human features.

Details

Coastal Region	Central Valley Region	Mountain Region	Desert Region
The Coastal Region has low mountains, a rocky coastline, broad valleys, and islands.			

 CALIFORNIA STANDARDS HSS 4.1, 4.1.3, 4.1.4; HI 2

12 ▪ Homework and Practice Book   Use after reading Chapter 1, pages 12–47.

© Harcourt

The First Californians

DIRECTIONS Read and answer the questions below about the first Californians.

1 What was California's climate like when the earliest people lived there?

_____

_____

2 How did the earliest Californians use mammoths?

_____

_____

3 What foods did the early Californians eat after the large animals died out?

_____

_____

4 What can we learn about early California Indians from the artifacts they left behind?

_____

_____

_____

© Harcourt

CALIFORNIA STANDARDS HSS 4.2, 4.2.1   *(continued)*

DIRECTIONS The early California Indians told legends, or stories, about how everything in the world came to be. These legends explained things that happened in nature and told about a tribe's history. Use the prewriting exercise below to help you develop a legend of your own. Your legend will tell about what caused the climate of California to become warmer and how it affected the lives of the California Indians.

My legend will be about

_____

Who will be the main character(s) in your legend?

_____

_____

What event will cause the climate change?

_____

_____

Write your own legend. Remember to describe the lives of California Indians at the beginning of the legend and at the end. Tell how their lives changed.

_____

_____

_____

_____

_____

_____

_____

_____

© Harcourt

Name _____ Date _____

The Northern Coastal Region

DIRECTIONS Fill in the blanks in the outline below to tell about the Indians of the northern Coastal Region. Use the terms below.

Yurok and Hupa	Pomo
planks	women
sweat lodge	coast
villages	brush
shaman	baskets
	men

I. Yurok and Hupa

    A. These Indians built their _____ along the Trinity and Klamath Rivers and the Pacific Ocean.

    B. Both the Yurok and Hupa used wooden _____ to build their houses, gathered acorns, and ate salmon.

    C. The Yurok had a religious leader called a _____. This leader would honor Nepewo in the First Salmon Ceremony.

    D. Hupa men gathered to think and pray inside a _____.

II. Pomo

    A. Some of these Indians built their villages along the _____ of California. Others from this group lived inland.

    B. Some Pomo Indians lived in houses shaped like cones. Others lived in large houses made from pole frames and covered with _____.

    C. Pomo _____ hunted and fished. Pomo _____ and children gathered nuts and berries.

    D. The Pomo were well known for their beautiful _____.

© Harcourt

CALIFORNIA STANDARDS HSS 4.2, 4.2.1

(continued)

Name _____ Date _____

DIRECTIONS Compare the Indians of the northern Coastal Region. Use the phrases listed below to complete the diagram. Use each phrase only once. Remember, if you write a phrase in the part where two ovals meet, it must be true for both of the tribes.

- Lived along the Trinity River
- Used sweat lodges
- Used weirs to catch fish
- Lived in plank houses
- Honored Nepewo in the First Salmon Ceremony
- Used natural resources
- Ate salmon and acorns
- Lived along the Klamath River and the Pacific Ocean

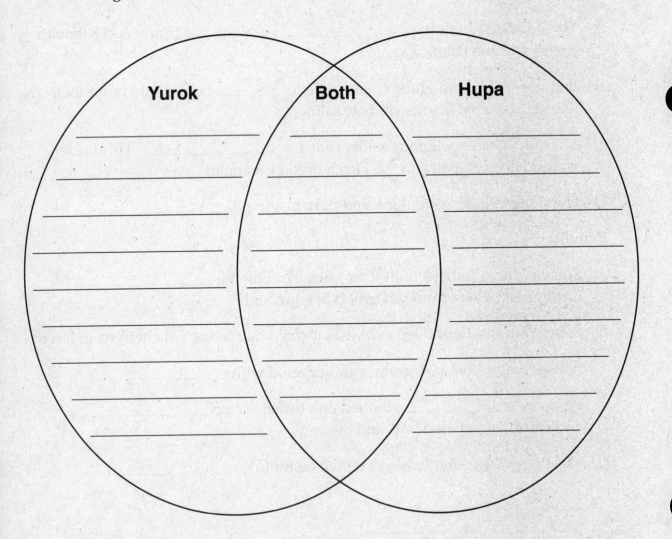

Yurok   Both   Hupa

Use after reading Chapter 2, Lesson 2, pages 62–67.

© Harcourt

Name _____ Date _____

The Southern Coastal Region

DIRECTIONS Pretend you are a Chumash boy or girl. Draw a picture of your village as if you are creating rock art. Then write a brief paragraph explaining the items in your pictograph. Be sure to indicate items that your people have obtained from the land and sea.

_____
_____
_____
_____
_____
_____
_____

CALIFORNIA STANDARDS HSS 4.1, 4.1.3, 4.2, 4.2.1

Skills: Compare Tables

Table A: Tribes, Regions, and Building Materials		
Tribe	**Region**	**Kinds of Building Materials for Houses**
Yurok	Northern Coastal	Wooden planks
Hupa	Northern Coastal	Wooden planks
Pomo	Northern Coastal	Wooden frame with bark; wooden frame with brush, grass, or other plant material
Chumash	Southern Coastal	Wooden frame with tule (marsh plant)
Maidu	Central Valley and Mountains	Wooden frame with bark; wooden frame with brush and dirt
Miwok	Central Valley and Mountains	Wooden frame with grass or tule; slabs of bark
Yokuts	Central Valley and Mountains	Wooden frame with brush or tule
Mojave	Desert	Wooden frame with brush, grass, or other plant material

Table B: Building Materials and Tribes	
Kinds of Building Materials for Houses	**Tribe**
Wooden planks	Yurok, Hupa
Wooden frame with bark	Pomo, Maidu
Slabs of bark	Miwok
Wooden frame with brush, grass, or other plant material	Pomo, Chumash, Maidu, Miwok, Yokuts, Mojave

© Harcourt

CALIFORNIA STANDARDS HSS 4.1, 4.1.5, 4.2, 4.2.1

(continued)

Name _____ Date _____

DIRECTIONS Compare the two tables on page 18. Then answer the questions below.

1 How does Table A organize the information?

_____

2 How does Table B organize the information?

_____

3 Which table is easier to use if you want to know which tribes built wooden frame houses covered with bark?

_____

4 Which table is easier to use if you wanted to know the kinds of building materials used by the Pomo Indians?

_____

DIRECTIONS For questions 5–10, write *A* for Table A and *B* for Table B in the space provided.

5 _____ Which table would you use to find information about the houses built by the Chumash Indians?

6 _____ Which table would you use for a report on how Indians in the northern Coastal Region of California used natural resources to build houses?

7 _____ Which table would you use to figure out which California Indian tribe built their houses from only bark?

8 _____ Which table would you use to find out which tribes used grass to build houses?

9 _____ Which table would you use to find out which tribes built their houses from wood planks?

10 _____ Which table would you use to tell how the Miwok Indians built their houses?

© Harcourt

Name _____ Date _____

The Central Valley and Mountains

DIRECTIONS Read the paragraphs below about the Indians of California's Central Valley and Mountain Regions. Circle the word or phrase that makes each sentence correct.

At one time, more than half of California's Indians may have lived in the Desert / Central Valley and Mountain Regions. This large population was easily supported because there was plenty of food and a comfortable climate.

The Maidu / Miwok lived mainly along the tributaries of the Sacramento River. Village groups were made up of several villages—usually about three to five villages / houses around a main village. The people stored extra baskets / acorns in a special building called a granary.

The Yokuts / Miwok lived north of San Francisco on the coast, on the eastern / western slopes of the Sierra Nevada, in the San Joaquin Valley, and near Mount Diablo. The children enjoyed playing games that helped them develop gathering / hunting skills.

The Yokuts / Miwok lived in the San Joaquin Valley and the foothills of the Sierra Nevada. They used wood from oak / palm trees to build their homes. The people of this tribe were excellent farmers / hunters, even though meat was not a large part of their diet.

© Harcourt

Name _____ Date _____

The Desert Region

DIRECTIONS Read the sentences listed below. Decide whether a statement might have been said by a Cahuilla Indian, a Mojave Indian, neither, or both. Write *C* for Cahuilla Indian, *M* for Mojave Indian, *N* for neither, or *B* for both.

1 _____ I live in the foothills of the San Bernardino Mountains.

2 _____ In the summer, my house has no walls.

3 _____ Sometimes I run all the way to the Pacific coast to trade.

4 _____ Many trees and plants grow nearby.

5 _____ I live in the valleys of the San Jacinto Mountains.

6 _____ Food is hard to find in my area because large animals are scarce and not much grows there.

7 _____ My people travel to help gather food.

8 _____ Each year, my people leave our village to gather acorns.

9 _____ I live in a dome-shaped house.

10 _____ I live near the Colorado River.

11 _____ Food is plentiful in my region of California.

12 _____ In my village, a granary on a platform is used to store food through the winter.

13 _____ I grow melons and pumpkins.

14 _____ I make clay pots.

15 _____ My village trades for what it needs.

© Harcourt

CALIFORNIA STANDARDS HSS 4.2, 4.2.1

Chapter 2

Name _____   Date _____

Study Guide

DIRECTIONS Louisa is making cards for a classroom display about California's Indians. Use the terms below to fill in the missing words.

Lesson 1	Lesson 2	Lesson 3	Lesson 4	Lesson 5
ancestors	shaman	government	granary	springs
tribes	ceremony	cooperate	division of	arid
culture	weirs	tomols	labor	silt
artifacts	trade	tar	specialize	resources
legends	plank			mountain areas

Lesson 1   The first groups, or _____, of Indians formed in

California about 4,000 years ago. Scientists study _____

these people left behind, such as clothing and tools. Each group

had its own _____, or way of life. They told

_____, or stories, which explained how things came

to be. These people were the _____ of present-day

American Indians.

Lesson 2   Indians of the northern Coastal Region could easily find food. The

Yurok used "fences" called _____ to catch salmon. A

Yurok religious leader called a _____ caught and ate the

first salmon during a _____. Northern Coastal Indians

used trees to make _____ houses. To get things they

could not make or find themselves, they would _____

valuable objects.

🐻 **CALIFORNIA STANDARDS HSS 4.1, 4.1.3, 4.2, 4.2.1**   (continued)

22 ■ Homework and Practice Book   Use after reading Chapter 2, pages 56–89.

© Harcourt

Name _____ Date _____

Lesson 3 The southern Coastal Region was home to many groups of Indians.

The Chumash lived along the Pacific Ocean and built _____

for water travel. They used _____ to make their

baskets and canoes waterproof. Like other Indians, the Chumash had a

_____ to help their people make rules and choose leaders.

Leaders encouraged their villages to _____ with one

another.

Lesson 4 At one time, more than half of California's Indians lived in

the Central Valley and Mountain Regions. Many Maidu villages had

a _____ to store extra acorns. The Maidu used a

_____ , or system of work, to help meet the needs of the

village. People would _____ at one kind of job to do it well.

Lesson 5 The fewest people lived in the Desert Region. Often, the

people there would go to _____ to gather food and

_____ . The Cahuilla lived near areas where water

came through openings in the ground called _____ . The

Mojave lived in dry, or _____ , land. However, they

lived near the Colorado River. When the river overflowed, it left behind

_____ , which allowed the Mojave to grow crops.

Name _____ Date _____

READING SOCIAL STUDIES: MAIN IDEA AND DETAILS

⭐ California's Indians

DIRECTIONS Complete the graphic organizer below to show that you understand important ideas and details about how California Indians lived.

Main Idea

California Indians adapted to their environment and used the natural resources around them to meet their needs.

Details

Indians in the Northern Coastal Region	Indians in the Southern Coastal Region	Indians in the Central Valley and Mountain Regions	Indians in the Desert Region
used trees to			
build shelters			
and boats			

© Harcourt

CALIFORNIA STANDARDS HSS 4.1, 4.1.3, 4.2, 4.2.1

Explorers Come to California

DIRECTIONS Imagine you are Hernando Cortés writing a letter to the Spanish monarch. You want to persuade him to fund an expedition to lands in the Americas. Fill in the blanks in the letter below to describe the benefits that the expedition would have for Spain.

Your Royal Majesty,

    I am writing this letter to tell you why it is so important to explore the American lands. I am a _____, an explorer and conqueror.

I want to travel to the lands known as _____ and bring glory to Spain.
    One benefit of my journey is that we may find a shortcut

to _____. Then it will be easier to _____ for silk and spices. I have heard stories about a narrow waterway called

the _____ of Anián, which may connect the Atlantic and

_____ Oceans. If we find this shortcut, we will no longer

have to sail around South America or _____ to reach Asia. This will save us time and will be much less dangerous.
    We could also become very rich. One group of native people in Mexico,

called the _____, has riches beyond belief. We could bring

back valuable _____, silver, and jewels.
    Another important reason to go to these new lands is that we

could help _____ the native people to Christianity.
    I hope you will honor my request.

Your humble servant,
Hernando Cortés

CALIFORNIA STANDARDS HSS 4.2, 4.2.2

Skills: Follow Routes on a Historical Map

DIRECTIONS Look at the map of Sir Francis Drake's voyages, below. Use the map to answer the questions.

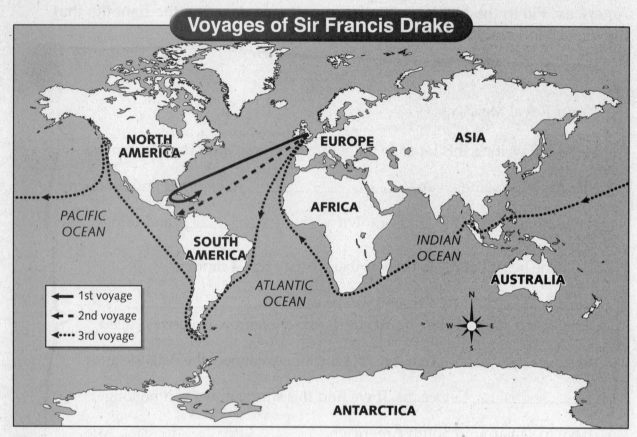

Voyages of Sir Francis Drake

1 On his first voyage, did Drake sail to North America?

_____

2 On his second voyage, did Drake sail to Asia?

_____

3 Which oceans did Drake sail across on his third voyage?

_____

4 After leaving on his first voyage, in which direction did Drake travel?

_____

5 On which voyage did Drake sail the farthest?

_____

 CALIFORNIA STANDARDS HSS 4.2, 4.2.2; CS 4

26 ■ **Homework and Practice Book**   Use after reading Chapter 3, Skill Lesson, pages 116–117.

© Harcourt

Newcomers to Alta California

DIRECTIONS Read each sentence about newcomers to Alta California. Decide whether each statement is true (*T*) or false (*F*).

1 _____ The first colonies in Alta California were started in the mid-1800s.

2 _____ In California, Catholic priests and other church workers served as missionaries.

3 _____ Junípero Serra founded the first missions in Alta California near San Diego Bay and Monterey Bay.

4 _____ The first expeditions to Alta California came only by land.

5 _____ The journey to Alta California by land was easy because of the flat, grassy land and cool weather.

6 _____ Juan Bautista de Anza found an easy land route to Alta California across northern Mexico.

7 _____ Gaspar de Portolá arrived at Monterey Bay on May 24, 1770.

8 _____ The decision to start a colony in Alta California came about because the Spanish were worried that Russian fur traders might move south along the coast and into Alta California.

9 _____ Before starting a colony in Alta California, Spain had already started colonies in what would become New York, Michigan, and Illinois.

10 _____ Missionaries tried to convert California Indians to the Catholic religion and teach them the Spanish language.

© Harcourt

CALIFORNIA STANDARDS HSS 4.2, 4.2.2, 4.2.3

Skills: Compare Primary and Secondary Sources

DIRECTIONS Study the sources listed below. Write whether the source is a primary source (*P*) or a secondary source (*S*).

1 _____ An encyclopedia entry about the history of California

2 _____ The diary of Sir Francis Drake

3 _____ Your friend's drawing of what he saw on his visit to a mission

4 _____ An interview with Juan Bautista de Anza after he reached Monterey

5 _____ A newspaper article about the death of Father Serra

6 _____ A painting of Hernando Cortés painted in 1975

7 _____ The autobiography of a conquistador

8 _____ A magazine article about California Indians

9 _____ A letter from a missionary in Monterey Bay to his brother in Spain

10 _____ Your social studies book

11 _____ The birth certificate of Gaspar de Portolá

12 _____ A copy of a speech given by King Carlos III announcing that Spain was starting colonies in Alta California

13 _____ A website about Spanish galleons

14 _____ An almanac entry about the population of California

15 _____ A television show about California explorers

CALIFORNIA STANDARDS HR 1

© Harcourt

Other Kinds of Settlements

DIRECTIONS Each of the statements below tells about a type of California settlement. Identify which kind of settlement a statement describes. Write *missions*, *presidios*, or *pueblos* on the line provided.

_____ **1** These forts were often built on natural harbors.

_____ **2** These had important buildings bordering a plaza.

_____ **3** These religious settlements were connected by El Camino Real.

_____ **4** These were usually located near fertile soil and fresh water.

_____ **5** The first one of these settlements was San José de Guadalupe.

_____ **6** These were built to protect settlements.

_____ **7** Each one had an *alcalde*, or mayor.

_____ **8** The people at these brought Christianity to the Indians.

_____ **9** Soldiers who lived at these settlements had many duties, such as hunting, working in the fields, caring for livestock, building and repairing structures, and delivering mail.

_____ **10** The people who lived at these farming communities grew food for the soldiers.

_____ **11** There were four of these—one near San Diego Bay, one in Santa Barbara, one in Monterey, and one in San Francisco.

_____ **12** Each of these was about a day's walk from the next one.

_____ **13** The name for these settlements means "village."

_____ **14** These were built in the shape of a square around an open courtyard where soldiers gathered.

_____ **15** San Jose, Los Angeles, and Santa Cruz each started out as one of these.

© Harcourt

CALIFORNIA STANDARDS HSS 4.2, 4.2.3, 4.2.4, 4.2.5

Skills: Read a Time Line

DIRECTIONS Review the details about the Spanish settlement of California from Lessons 2 and 3 of your textbook. Write the year in which each of the events happened. Then place the question number for each event in the correct order on the time line shown on the next page.

_____ **1** George Vancouver visits the San Francisco presidio.

_____ **2** The pueblo of Santa Cruz is built.

_____ **3** Priests begin setting up missions.

_____ **4** The pueblo that will become Los Angeles is founded.

_____ **5** The settlement of Alta California's first pueblo, San José de Guadalupe, occurs.

_____ **6** At this time, only 600 settlers live in Alta California.

_____ **7** The first presidio in Alta California is built near San Diego Bay.

_____ **8** The second pueblo is settled near Mission San Gabriel.

_____ **9** Juan Bautista de Anza and a group of 240 settlers reach Monterey.

_____ **10** The last of 21 missions is founded.

© Harcourt

CALIFORNIA STANDARDS HSS 4.2, 4.2.3, 4.2.4; CS 1, 2   *(continued)*

Name _____ Date _____

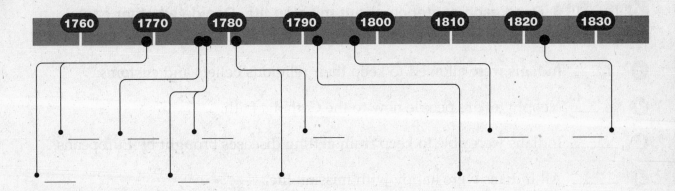

1 How many years are there between each date on the time line above?

_____

2 Which two centuries are shown on the time line?

_____

_____

3 During which decade did the most events take place?

_____

4 Which came first, pueblos or presidios? How do you know?

_____

_____

5 How many years were there between the founding of the first and last missions?

_____

© Harcourt

Mission Life

DIRECTIONS Read each sentence about mission life. Decide whether each statement is true (*T*) or false (*F*).

1 _____ Indians were allowed to keep their religious beliefs and customs.

2 _____ Neophytes are people new to the Catholic faith.

3 _____ Indians were able to keep from getting diseases brought by Europeans.

4 _____ All Indians were happy with mission life.

5 _____ Indians at the missions spent little time working or praying.

6 _____ Before they lived at missions, most Indians were hunters and gatherers.

7 _____ The mission system changed the economy of California.

8 _____ Missions used a bugle to call people to prayer and work.

9 _____ Nicolas José and Toypurina planned a revolt at a mission.

10 _____ All California Indians were farmers before the arrival of the Franciscan priests.

11 _____ Some Indians were forced to go to the missions by soldiers.

12 _____ Some Indians were taught about carpentry and metalworking at missions.

13 _____ Indian children were not allowed to go to school at the missions.

14 _____ Mission Indians were not allowed to wear their traditional clothing.

15 _____ During the 75 years after the first missions, the Indian population nearly doubled.

© Harcourt

CALIFORNIA STANDARDS HSS 4.2, 4.2.4, 4.2.5, 4.2.6

Chapter 3

Name _____ Date _____

Study Guide

DIRECTIONS Kyle is writing a letter to Lucas, who will move to California soon. Kyle has been telling Lucas about the history of California. Help him finish this letter by filling in the blanks with words from the lists below.

Lesson 1		Lesson 2	Lesson 3	Lesson 4
conquistadors	ocean currents	colony	presidio	economy
costs	wind patterns	missions	pueblo	neophytes
benefits	land	missionary	plaza	revolted
peninsula	trade	Spain	*alcalde*	customs
galleons	shortcut	Alta California	judge	forced

Dear Lucas,

Lesson 1   Here is your next letter about California's history. The earliest

Spanish explorers were known as _____ because they

conquered as they explored. They wanted to claim _____

and riches for Spain. Some explorers wanted to find a _____

to Asia. They knew that the _____ would be high, but they

believed that the _____ were great. It would shorten the trip to

Asia, making _____ with Asia easier. While looking for a trade

route, Hernando Cortés reached what he thought was an island, but it was

really a _____ . Ships called _____ made quick

trips to Asia from New Spain, thanks to the _____ and the

_____ in the Pacific Ocean.

© Harcourt

Name _____ Date _____

Lesson 2   To protect its claims in _____ from other countries, Spain started a _____. The king of _____ did this by building _____, or religious settlements. A person who teaches religion to others at a mission is called a _____.

Lesson 3   There were also other kinds of settlements in Alta California. One kind was a farming community called a _____. This type of community was built around an open square called a _____, where people could gather. Each community had a mayor who also served as a _____. This person was called an _____. Another kind of settlement was a _____. These settlements were built for protection.

Lesson 4   The missions changed the _____ of Alta California to one based on farming. They changed the lives of the Indians as well. Some Indians went to the missions because they wanted to. Other Indians were _____ to go to the missions. At the missions, Indians had to give up their traditional ways of life. They became _____ to the Catholic faith. Some Indians were so unhappy that they _____ against the missions. Indians did not want to give up their traditional beliefs and _____.

That's it for now! I hope you enjoy California's history as much as I do!
Your friend,
Kyle

© Harcourt

READING SOCIAL STUDIES: GENERALIZE

(Focus Skill) Exploration and Early Settlements

DIRECTIONS Complete the graphic organizer with facts to show that you understand the facts and can generalize about European exploration and early settlement of California.

Facts

The Spanish explorer Cabrillo reaches San Diego Bay.			

Generalization

Over time, the Europeans explored California, and the Spanish established missions to settle California.

CALIFORNIA STANDARDS HSS 4.2, 4.2.2, 4.2.3; HI 1

Name _____ Date _____

Mexico Wins Its Freedom

DIRECTIONS September 16, 1810, marked an important day for Mexico. That was the day the Mexican War for Independence began. Fill in the blanks in the outline below to explain some of the reasons for this war and its effects on California. Use the terms below.

independence	mestizos	Dolores	secularization
Indians	Californios	economy	criollos

I. Dislike of the Spanish government caused the war.

    A. People born of Spanish parents in Mexico,

       or _____, were not treated as equals of people born in Spain.

    B. Other groups that suffered from unequal treatment were Indians and

       _____, or people of both European and Indian heritage.

    C. Mexicans wanted _____, or freedom, from Spanish rule.

    D. Father Miguel Hidalgo y Costilla gave a famous speech called "the Cry of

       _____."

II. Mexican rule affected California.

    A. Most Spanish-speaking people of Alta

       California, or _____,
       welcomed Mexican rule.

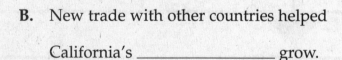

    B. New trade with other countries helped

       California's _____ grow.

    C. The Mexican government ordered _____, or ended church
       rule, of the missions.

    D. When the missions closed, the _____ got very little mission
       land.

© Harcourt

 CALIFORNIA STANDARDS HSS 4.2, 4.2.7, 4.2.8; HI 3   *(continued)*

36 ▪ **Homework and Practice Book**   Use after reading Chapter 4, Lesson 1, pages 148–153.

Name _____ Date _____

1 We were promised mission land after the end of the Mexican War for Independence. Instead, Californios and new settlers became the owners of most of the land. We often have no choice but to work for them.

This is the viewpoint of the _____ .

2 Now that the war is over, we will allow ships from many countries, including the United States, to sail into California harbors.

This is the viewpoint of the _____ .

3 The fighting in Mexico is taking all of our resources. The soldiers in the presidios will have to find their own supplies.

This is the viewpoint of the _____ .

4 We're glad we ended the church rule of the missions. Now the people of California can own this good land.

This is the viewpoint of the _____ .

5 People who were not born in Spain and people of both European and Indian heritage should not hold good jobs in our government or in the church.

This is the viewpoint of the _____ .

Skills: Identify Multiple Causes and Effects

DIRECTIONS Read the paragraph below. Then answer the questions.

Julie had a test on Mexican rule in California. She wanted to do well on the test, so she decided to study carefully. Her mother asked her if she would like to go to the library to use its books as well. Julie said she would. When Julie told some of her classmates that she was going to the library to study, they decided to go with her. Julie and her classmates studied carefully for the test. When Julie took the test, she got a perfect score of 100. She will get an *A* in social studies. Because of getting an *A*, she will have the grades she needs to make the honor roll this semester. This has made Julie very happy. Her parents are also very proud of her for working so hard.

1 Was Julie's studying for her test a cause or an effect of her getting a perfect score?

_____

2 When Julie's classmates went to the library, was that a cause or an effect of Julie's decision to study in the library?

_____

3 What were the two causes of Julie's doing well on her test?

_____

4 What was the next effect after Julie found out she would get an *A* in social studies?

_____

5 What were the two effects of Julie's making the honor roll?

_____

© Harcourt

CALIFORNIA STANDARDS HSS 4.2, 4.2.7, 4.2.8; HI 3   *(continued)*

Name _____ Date _____

Use information from Lesson 1 to complete the diagram. Show the multiple causes and effects on California of Mexican independence.

Cause
Mexico wins independence.

↓

Effect
Mexican laws and officials are put in place in _____.

Cause	Cause
The _____ government changes the trading laws.	The _____ system comes to an end in California.

↓ ↓

Effects	Effects
• _____ from many countries begin sailing into California's harbors. • An increase in trade helps California's _____ to grow.	• The Indians get little of the _____ that the Mexican government promised them. • Many Indians have to work for _____ because they do not know how to live outside the missions.

© Harcourt

Use after reading Chapter 4, Skill Lesson, pages 154–155.   **Homework and Practice Book ■ 39**

Rise of the Rancho Economy

DIRECTIONS Read the paragraph about haciendas. Use the information from the paragraph to answer the questions.

Haciendas were usually large, one-story houses. They were made from sun-dried bricks called adobe. The roof of a hacienda was made of tile. A hacienda was built around a big, open courtyard. Arched hallways were found throughout the building. The kitchen of the hacienda was in a separate building. It was located away from the main house to prevent fires from destroying the hacienda. Haciendas were often used to host large celebrations, such as weddings and harvest festivals. Over time, many former haciendas were changed into hotels. Some of these haciendas still exist today.

1 How many stories did a hacienda have?

_____

2 What materials were used to build a hacienda?

_____

3 Why was the kitchen away from the main house?

_____

_____

4 What was the house built around?

_____

5 What kinds of parties might be held at a hacienda?

_____

_____

© Harcourt

CALIFORNIA STANDARDS HSS 4.2, 4.2.5, 4.2.8; CS 1   *(continued)*

Name _____ Date _____

DIRECTIONS Read the sentences below. Then write the numbers 1 to 5 in the blanks to put the sentences in the correct order. The first one has been done for you.

Mariano Vallejo made tallow candles at Rancho Petaluma, in northern California. The tallow, or beef fat, came from cattle raised at the mission. Even though the candles were very useful, many people didn't like to use them. Tallow candles burned unevenly, were smoky, and had a strong smell. Because they were made of animal fat the candles could melt in very hot weather, and mice loved to nibble on them.

Making Tallow Candles

_____ The workers let the tallow on the wicks become cool and hard. Then the workers turn the wheel and dip all the candles again. The candles may need to be dipped several times until they are large enough to use.

__1__ The candle makers build a hot fire and melt tallow in a large container. They tie candlewicks to wooden frames hanging from the spokes of the candle-making wheel.

_____ The candle makers store the finished candles in a cool, mouse-proof place.

_____ Then a worker turns the candle-making wheel and dips each set of wicks until all the wicks are coated with tallow.

_____ Using ropes that raise and lower the frames of hanging wicks, a worker dips the first row of hanging wicks into the melted tallow.

© Harcourt

Life on the Ranchos

DIRECTIONS Read the sentences about life on the ranchos. Write *T* next to the statements that are true and *F* next to the statements that are false.

1 _____ The main job of the vaquero was to round up a rancho's cattle as they wandered around the countryside.

2 _____ A brand is the kind of clothing a vaquero wore when riding a horse to gather cattle.

3 _____ A good vaquero could catch any animal by throwing a reata and looping it around the animal's neck.

4 _____ A reata is a large, wooden harness with a hole in the center.

5 _____ Some women ran their own ranchos and worked with the cattle.

6 _____ Indians worked as vaqueros, cooks, and farmers.

7 _____ Most Indians earned money for the work they did on a rancho.

8 _____ At social events, such as fiestas, vaqueros often participated in horse races or bullfights.

9 _____ Usually one small family lived in the hacienda of a rancho.

10 _____ Public schools were available for the children on the rancho to attend.

© Harcourt

CALIFORNIA STANDARDS HSS 4.2, 4.2.5, 4.2.8   *(continued)*

Name _____ Date _____

DIRECTIONS There was always much work to do on the rancho. Everyone had to help out. Read the paragraphs below. Then identify whether the paragraph is describing *a vaquero*, *a rancho owner*, or *an Indian worker*.

1 People are waking up very early for work on a rancho. One worker feeds a horse before eating breakfast. The worker is wearing a short jacket over a shirt and pants. This worker is very skilled in using a reata. The worker spends most of the day rounding up the rancho's cattle. The pay for this work will be spent on things the worker needs.

The worker is _____.

2 A fiesta is being held at the rancho. Everyone on the rancho is busy preparing for the many guests who are coming to celebrate a wedding. One woman oversees all of the workers and makes sure the rancho is prepared for a week-long fiesta. This woman is very wealthy and can afford to feed and entertain many guests at the wedding celebration.

The woman is _____.

3 Riders are working hard to round up cattle. One of the workers will ride many miles today. This skillful rider works hard to do a good job. In exchange for this hard work the rider receives food, some clothes, and a place to live.

The rider is _____.

4 Life on a rancho is very busy. There is a worker who works as a cook and also in the fields as a farmer. At the end of this busy day, the worker goes home to a small village. The village is right on the rancho.

The worker is _____.

5 Tonight there is a fiesta at the rancho, with many guests. One guest attends the fiesta after being paid for rounding up cattle. The guest is a skillful horse rider. Wearing a loose shirt, pants, and a short jacket, the guest wins a horse race at the fiesta.

The guest is _____.

Chapter 4

Name _____ Date _____

Study Guide

DIRECTIONS Jessica wrote a book report for history class. The book she read told about life in California before and after Mexico gained its freedom from Spain. Fill in the missing words in Jessica's report. Use the terms below.

Lesson 1	Lesson 2		Lesson 3
criollos	barter	tallow	vaqueros
secularization	economy	Mexican	labor
independence	hacienda	Californios	fiestas
Mexicans	ranchos	land grants	reata
mestizos	diseño	ports	brand

Lesson 1   I read a book about life in California before and after Mexico

gained its freedom from Spain. The first part of the book told about what

led up to the war and what happened afterward. Many _____

did not like being ruled by Spain. Under Spain's rule, people born in

Mexico of Spanish parents, the _____, could not hold

good jobs. Spain treated people of both European and Indian heritage,

the _____, even worse. Mexico fought a war to win its

_____ from Spain. After the war, most of the Spanish-

speaking people of Alta California, the Californios, welcomed Mexican rule.

The new government ended the church-ruled mission system in California

and ordered the _____ of the missions.

CALIFORNIA STANDARDS HSS 4.2, 4.2.5, 4.2.7, 4.2.8   *(continued)*

© Harcourt

Lesson 2   The second part of the book told of life in California in that

time. To attract people to California, the _____ government

offered gifts of land, or _____ . If someone wanted land, he

or she wrote a letter that included a hand-drawn map. The map, called

a _____ , showed the boundaries of the land. Many settlers

started large cattle ranches, called _____ . These had a main

house, called a _____ , and pasture for cattle and horses.

Before the war, the _____ of California were closed to foreign

ships. Once ships were allowed to dock, trade became important to the

_____ . When a ship arrived, people would _____

one item for another. Traders wanted _____ to make soap and

candles. The Spanish-speaking people of California, the _____ ,

needed things they could not get in California.

Lesson 3   Life on a rancho was very interesting. There was always

much work, or _____ , to be done. Cowhands called

_____ were skilled at using a rope called a _____

to round up the rancho's cattle. Sometimes these workers would mark

young cattle with a _____ to show the cattle belonged to that

rancho. Even with all the work, people on the ranchos still found time to

celebrate. Large parties, or _____ , could last for days, and

people traveled from far away to attend. I think I would have liked to live on

a rancho during this time and to have joined the riders on their long rides.

READING SOCIAL STUDIES: GENERALIZE

⭐ (Focus Skill) Mexican Rule in California

DIRECTIONS Complete the graphic organizer with facts to show that you understand the facts and can generalize about the settlement of Mexican California from the early 1800s to 1850.

Facts

Mexico won its independence from Spain.			
	_____	_____	_____
	_____	_____	_____
	_____	_____	_____
	_____	_____	_____
	_____	_____	_____
	_____	_____	_____
	_____	_____	_____
	_____	_____	_____
	_____	_____	_____
	_____	_____	_____
	_____	_____	_____
	_____	_____	_____
	_____	_____	_____

Generalization

The economy of California grew stronger and its population increased under Mexican rule.

© Harcourt

CALIFORNIA STANDARDS HSS 4.2, 4.2.8; HI 1

Americans Move West

DIRECTIONS Read the paragraphs below about the expeditions of different explorers. Decide which explorer might have given each description and write his name in the space provided.

James Beckwourth

James Ohio Pattie

Jedediah Strong Smith

Joseph Reddeford Walker

Ewing Young

Jedediah Strong Smith

1 In 1826, I led 17 men on a trapping expedition. Our expedition left from the Great Salt Lake area. We headed southwest and eventually reached the Colorado River. Then we made our way across the Mojave Desert.

I am _____.

2 My father and I began an expedition in 1827. We were not welcome in California. We were put in jail. I was later freed, but my father died in jail.

I am _____..

3 My travels in the 1830s helped develop the Old Spanish Trail. It ran from Santa Fe, New Mexico, to southern California.

I am _____.

4 I was the first American to cross the Sierra Nevada from the east. I found a pass through the mountains. The pass was later named after me.

I am _____.

5 In 1850, I found a new pass through the northern Sierra Nevada. The pass was later named after me.

I am _____.

© Harcourt

 CALIFORNIA STANDARDS HSS 4.3, 4.3.2

Name _____ Date _____

Skills: Distinguish Fact from Opinion

DIRECTIONS Read the following statements. Decide if the statements are fact (*F*) or opinion (*O*).

1 _____ By the 1820s, the supply of beavers was almost used up in the United States.

2 _____ Ewing Young was the bravest trailblazer because he helped develop the Old Spanish Trail.

3 _____ Father José Bernardo Sánchez was a nice person because he gave Jedediah Strong Smith's men food and a place to stay.

4 _____ American trappers moved west to find fur-bearing animals.

5 _____ The Walker Pass is the easiest way to cross the Sierra Nevada.

6 _____ In 1826, Jedediah Strong Smith led 17 men on a trapping expedition.

7 _____ It was wrong to put James Ohio Pattie and his father, Sylvester Pattie, in jail.

8 _____ California was the best place in all of North America to trap beavers and other animals.

9 _____ Jedediah Strong Smith was one of the first people from the United States to travel to Alta California by land.

10 _____ James Ohio Pattie and his father, Sylvester Pattie, began an expedition to California in 1827.

© Harcourt

CALIFORNIA STANDARDS HSS 4.3, 4.3.2

(continued)

Name _____ Date _____

TRAPPERS, MOVE TO CALIFORNIA!

With the supply of beaver fur so low, and the demand high, people will pay high prices for furs! You will definitely become rich by trapping and selling furs! The journey to California will be difficult because of the deserts and steep mountains you will have to cross. Do you like adventure? You will become a famous trailblazer and find a new path for other people to follow.

1 "With the supply of beaver fur so low, and the demand high, people will pay high prices for furs!"

Is this a fact or an opinion? _____

2 "You will definitely become rich by trapping and selling furs!"

Is this a fact or an opinion? _____

3 "The journey to California will be difficult because of the deserts and steep mountains you will have to cross."

Is this a fact or an opinion? _____

4 "You will become a famous trailblazer and find a new path for other people to follow."

Is this a fact or an opinion? _____

5 Pretend you are a trapper. After reading this advertisement, would you move to California? Explain why or why not.

_____

_____

© Harcourt

Trails to California

DIRECTIONS Pioneers brought many supplies with them on their journey to California. Some possible supplies are listed below. Read each situation, which might have happened to you if you had traveled in a wagon train to California. Then study the list, decide which item you would leave behind, and cross it off the list. For each situation, you must choose from what you have left. Explain your choices on a separate sheet of paper.

Things to Bring to California		
bucket of grease for the wagon wheels	butter churn	axe
bucket of hot coals to start campfires	food	hammer
watertight wooden barrel	rifle	saw
pots and pans	extra clothing	plow
stove	blankets	seeds

1 First you must cross a flooded river. You will have to remove the wagon wheels and float the wagon across the river. The wagon is too heavy. What item do you leave behind?

2 Now you are struggling across the dry plains. Your animals are weak with thirst and are struggling to pull the wagon. What item do you leave behind to lighten the load?

3 American Indians meet your wagon train and want to trade with you. What items could you give them in trade? What might you want them to give you in return?

4 Your wagon train has reached the mountains. The climb is steep and the wagon is still too heavy for the oxen to pull up the slope. What item do you leave behind?

© Harcourt

CALIFORNIA STANDARDS HSS 4.3, 4.3.2

Skills: Distinguish Fact from Fiction

DIRECTIONS Many people kept journals and diaries as they traveled west. Read the excerpt below from John Bidwell's journal. Then answer the questions that follow.

This morning, the wagons started off in single file; first the four carts and one small wagon of the missionaries: next eight wagons drawn by mules and horses, and lastly, five wagons drawn by seventeen yoke [pair] of oxen. It was the calculation [plan] of the company to move on slowly till the wagon of Chiles overtook us. Our course was west. Leaving the Kansas no great distance to our left, we traveled in the valley of the river, which was prairie excepting near the margin [bank] of the stream. The day was very warm, and we stopped about noon, having traveled about twelve miles.

—from the journal of John Bidwell

1 Identify one fact from the excerpt above.

_____

2 How can you prove that something is a fact?

_____

3 What is one advantage and one disadvantage of using a documentary source, such as John Bidwell's journal?

_____

_____

_____

© Harcourt

DIRECTIONS Read these sentences from a fictional story about the Bartleson-Bidwell expedition. Use what you know about the expedition to decide which of the sentences give a *fact* about the expedition. Label all other sentences *fiction*. Then answer the question below.

Mr. Hopper Is Going West

1 _____ I spent the afternoon with my friend Mr. Hopper.

2 _____ Mr. Hopper will soon join the Bartleson-Bidwell expedition.

3 _____ The Bartleson-Bidwell expedition is going to California.

4 _____ The group has chosen John Bartleson to lead the trip west.

5 _____ The expedition will leave from Missouri in May 1841.

6 _____ The Bartleson-Bidwell expedition plans to follow the Oregon Trail on part of its trip to California.

7 _____ At some point, the expedition will have to leave the Oregon Trail and go southwest in order to get to California.

8 _____ Mr. Hopper is excited about going to California.

9 _____ He hopes to start a great rancho there.

10 _____ "There is land to be had in California," he says. "I will get a land grant."

11 _____ The government is giving land grants to new settlers in California.

12 _____ Mr. Hopper says he expects to reach California before winter arrives.

13 How does a fiction writer use facts and fiction in a historical story?

_____

_____

_____

_____

Americans in California

DIRECTIONS Read the statements about Americans in California. Decide whether each statement is true (*T*) or false (*F*).

James K. Polk

1 _____ Settlers in California could own land only if they were American citizens.

2 _____ The idea that the United States should expand to reach from the Atlantic Ocean to the Pacific Ocean was known as the Polk Doctrine.

3 _____ In 1845, President James K. Polk offered Mexico $40 million for what are now California, New Mexico, and Arizona.

4 _____ The Mexican government was able to stop settlers from moving to California.

5 _____ In 1846, a group of settlers from the United States marched into the town of San Francisco to take control of California away from Mexico.

6 _____ Squatters had the same rights and protections as Mexican citizens.

7 _____ In a republic, the people elect their own leaders.

8 _____ Mariano Vallejo thought that California would be better off separated from Mexico.

9 _____ A rebel is someone who fights against the government.

10 _____ All Californios were in agreement about being ruled by Mexico.

CALIFORNIA STANDARDS HSS 4.2, 4.2.8

The Mexican-American War

DIRECTIONS Number the sentences below from 1 through 10 to show the correct order of events.

_____ Mexican governor Pío Pico and General Andrés Pico arrange the surrender of California.

_____ The United States and Mexico sign the Treaty of Guadalupe Hidalgo, ending the Mexican-American War.

_____ Robert F. Stockton sends a group of the Bear Flaggers to take control of other California cities.

_____ John D. Sloat sails to Monterey and takes over the city.

_____ American troops fight the Californios at Domínguez Rancho, and the Californios win.

_____ Texas wins its independence from Mexico.

_____ Mexican and American leaders sign the Treaty of Cahuenga, ending the fighting in California.

_____ American troops cross the Texas-Mexico border, and Mexican troops attack them.

_____ Robert F. Stockton leaves Archibald Gillespie in charge of Los Angeles, and some Californios rebel.

_____ Californios surprise the American troops and win the Battle of San Pasqual.

1846

Present

CALIFORNIA STANDARDS HSS 4.3; CS 1

54 ▪ **Homework and Practice Book**   Use after reading Chapter 5, Lesson 4, pages 212–217.

Skills: Read and Compare Historical Maps

DIRECTIONS El Camino Real was a trail that connected missions, presidios, and pueblos in California. Today, U.S. Highway 101 connects California cities along a similar path. Study the two maps below. Then answer the questions.

1 South of Monterey, what waterway do both El Camino Real and U.S. Highway 101 generally follow?

_____

2 Which mission was once located near the present-day city of Sonoma?

_____

3 Which two cities on the map were once presidios?

_____

4 What former pueblo on the map is now a California city?

_____

© Harcourt

CALIFORNIA STANDARDS HSS 4.1, 4.1.4, 4.2, 4.2.4; CS 4

Chapter 5

Study Guide

DIRECTIONS Maria watched a documentary on television about how California became a state. The next day in school, she gave a report on the documentary to her class. Fill in the missing words in Maria's report. Use the terms below.

Lesson 1	Lesson 2	Lesson 3	Lesson 4
demand	wagon trains	Bear Flaggers	Monterey
passes	immigrants	squatters	treaty
frontier	pioneers	republic	Texas
trailblazers	California Trail	rebels	rights
supply	Sutter's Fort	manifest destiny	Domínguez Rancho

Lesson 1   Yesterday, I saw a documentary about how California became a

state. The documentary explained that in the 1820s, trappers went into the

_____ to find beavers. The price of beaver fur had gone up

because the _____ was high and the _____ was

low. As more trappers explored California, _____ found several

openings, or _____, through the mountains that made it easier

to travel west.

Lesson 2   Next, the documentary explained that many people from other

countries, called _____, came to California by ship.

_____ also traveled overland to California in groups of wagons

to be among the first settlers there. The groups of wagons were known as

_____. They often followed the main route to California, called

the _____. Many people stopped at _____ for

supplies or to find jobs.

CALIFORNIA STANDARDS HSS 4.2, 4.2.8, 4.3, 4.3.1, 4.3.2   *(continued)*

© Harcourt

Lesson 3   In the mid-1800s many people thought the United States should reach from the Atlantic Ocean to the Pacific Ocean. This idea was called _____. Some American settlers in California became Mexican citizens and owned their own land. Those who lived on land without permission were called _____. People disagreed on who should rule California. One group wanted to take control of California away from Mexico. The people who fought against the Mexican government were called _____. They wanted California to elect its own leaders and be a free _____. This group became known as the _____.

Lesson 4   The final part of the documentary explained the reasons for the Mexican-American War. One reason for the war was a disagreement about the border between Mexico and _____. The Americans saw the war as a way to take control of California. John D. Sloat sailed to the capital of Mexican California, which was _____. He said that California was now part of the United States. Sloat told Californians they would have the same freedoms, or _____, as United States citizens. Many battles followed, including one at _____ in Los Angeles. Finally, an agreement, or _____, was signed by the United States and Mexico. It stopped the fighting, and the United States gained ownership of California.

Name _____ Date _____

READING SOCIAL STUDIES: COMPARE AND CONTRAST
(Focus Skill) California, Here We Come!

DIRECTIONS Complete each Venn diagram to show that you understand how the journeys of trailblazers were alike and how they were different.

Topic 1

Smith

- started in 1826
- ordered to leave California

Similar

_____
_____
_____
_____
_____

Topic 2

Pattie

- started in 1827
- jailed by Governor Echeandía

Topic 1

Young

_____
_____
_____
_____

Similar

- both found routes into California that became important routes for trade and for settlers

Topic 2

Walker

_____
_____
_____
_____
_____
_____

 CALIFORNIA STANDARDS HSS 4.3, 4.3.2

Use after reading Chapter 5, pages 190–219.

© Harcourt

Name _____ Date _____

The Gold Rush

DIRECTIONS Complete the chart below about the advantages and disadvantages of routes to California. Then answer the questions that follow.

Route to California	Advantages	Disadvantages
Panama route	_____ _____	Disease, hot climate
All-water route	Cost the least	_____ _____
Overland route	_____ _____ _____ _____	_____ _____ _____ _____

If you were a forty-niner, which route would you take? Why?

_____

_____

_____

_____

_____

CALIFORNIA STANDARDS HSS 4.3, 4.3.2; HI 4

Name _____ Date _____

The Effects of the Gold Rush

DIRECTIONS Read the statements below. Decide whether each statement best describes entrepreneurs (*E*), miners (*M*), or California Indians (*I*).

1 _____ Women and African Americans in California often belonged to this group.

2 _____ Members of this group often earned a living by opening stores or hotels.

3 _____ Many people in this group eventually gave up on their dreams of finding gold but decided to stay in California anyway.

4 _____ The places where they hunted, fished, and gathered food were sometimes ruined by mining.

5 _____ The methods they used to do their jobs sometimes hurt the environment.

6 _____ Of the three groups, they often had the best chance of becoming rich.

7 _____ Members of this group came to seek gold but many thought that only people from the United States should look for gold in California.

8 _____ Levi Strauss was one of these people.

9 _____ They were often forced off their land by miners.

10 _____ These people set up new businesses.

11 _____ These people usually stayed in dirty camps with other forty-niners.

12 _____ It was sometimes said that they "mined the miners."

13 _____ These people sold goods and services.

14 _____ In this group, women could often make more money than men.

© Harcourt

CALIFORNIA STANDARDS HSS 4.3, 4.3.3, 4.3.4, 4.4, 4.4.2   *(continued)*

60 ■ Homework and Practice Book   Use after reading Chapter 6, Lesson 2, pages 236–243.

Name _____ Date _____

1 How did women benefit from the gold rush?

_____

_____

2 How were the towns of Stockton and Marysville changed by the gold rush?

_____

_____

3 How did hydraulic mining affect some California waterways?

_____

_____

4 Why did goods and services cost so much during the gold rush?

_____

_____

5 What did vigilantes do?

_____

_____

© Harcourt

Skills: Read a Line Graph

DIRECTIONS Study the line graphs of the populations of Los Angeles and Sacramento between the years 1850 and 1890. Use the graphs to answer the questions on the next page.

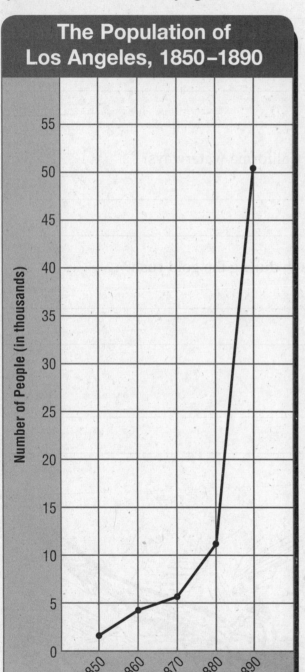

The Population of Los Angeles, 1850–1890

Number of People (in thousands) / Year

Source: California Department of Finance

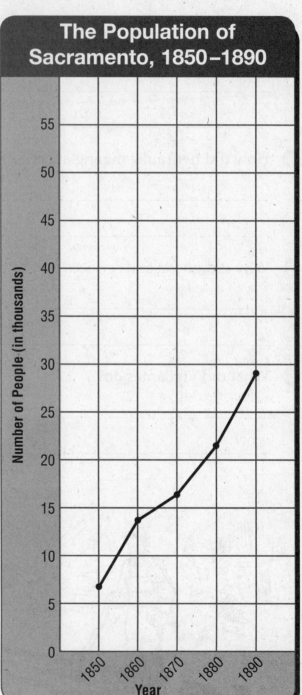

The Population of Sacramento, 1850–1890

Number of People (in thousands) / Year

CALIFORNIA STANDARDS HSS 4.4, 4.4.3, 4.4.4   *(continued)*

Name _____   Date _____

1 What does the line graph tell you about the population of Los Angeles between 1850 and 1890?

_____

_____

_____

2 Was Sacramento's population in 1870 greater than or less than 15,000?

_____

_____

3 About how many more people lived in Los Angeles in 1880 than in 1870?

_____

_____

4 About how many more people lived in Sacramento in 1890 than in 1880?

_____

_____

5 In 1890, about how many more people lived in Los Angeles than in Sacramento?

_____

_____

California Becomes a State

DIRECTIONS Pretend you are a delegate at the Monterey Convention being interviewed by a reporter. Answer the following questions from your interview.

1 Why are Californians holding this convention?

_____

_____

_____

2 How will the new government differ from past governments?

_____

_____

_____

3 Will you keep any laws from past governments?

_____

_____

4 How many delegates are there? Who is represented?

_____

_____

_____

5 What decisions does the Monterey Convention face?

_____

_____

_____

_____

© Harcourt

CALIFORNIA STANDARDS HSS 4.3, 4.3.5, 4.4, 4.4.8; CS 1   *(continued)*

64 ▪ **Homework and Practice Book**   Use after reading Chapter 6, Lesson 3, pages 246–252.

Name _____ Date _____

DIRECTIONS Using the numbers 1–10, place these events from California's journey to statehood in the correct order.

_____ California's two senators ask Congress to allow California to join the United States.

_____ The Monterey Convention takes place.

_____ Sacramento is chosen as the state capital.

_____ Peter H. Burnett is chosen to serve as the first state governor.

_____ The United States takes control of California.

_____ California officially becomes a state.

_____ The members of Congress agree on the Compromise of 1850.

_____ General Bennet Riley calls for a convention to make decisions about California's future.

_____ California is put under military rule.

_____ The people of California vote to ratify the new constitution.

Skills: Resolve Conflict

DIRECTIONS Answer the questions
below to help resolve a conflict.

Matt and Aisha are a brother and sister
with a problem. Matt wants to use the
craft table to make his social studies
project. Aisha wants to use the craft
table to make her science project.
What should they do?

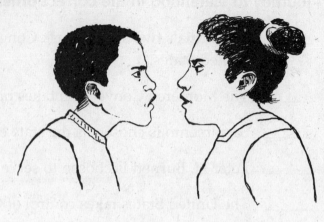

1 What is the conflict?

_____

_____

2 What does each person want?

_____

_____

3 How might Matt want to resolve the problem?

_____

_____

4 How might Aisha want to resolve the problem?

_____

_____

5 What compromise could Matt and Aisha find?

_____

_____

_____

_____

CALIFORNIA STANDARDS HSS 4.3   (continued)

Name _____ Date _____

DIRECTIONS The delegates to the Monterey Convention had many important decisions to make, such as where California's eastern border should be and whether or not California should be a free state. In the end, delegates chose to set the eastern border at the Sierra Nevada and the Colorado River and for California to be a free state. With 48 delegates, many other compromises must have been made to reach an agreement.

Think of a conflict that happened recently in your classroom, school, or community. Answer the questions below to describe the conflict and its resolution.

1 Describe the conflict.

_____

_____

2 What did each person want?

_____

_____

3 How did each person want to resolve the conflict?

_____

_____

4 How was the conflict resolved?

_____

_____

_____

5 What are some compromises that could have been made?

_____

_____

_____

© Harcourt

Chapter 6

Name _____ Date _____

Study Guide

DIRECTIONS Jessica is a reporter for her school's student newspaper. She decided to write an article to answer a reader's question, "How does the name of the San Francisco 49ers relate to California's history?" Use the terms below to fill in the missing words of her article.

Lesson 1	Lesson 2	Lesson 3
gold rush	consumers	convention
forty-niners	entrepreneurs	delegates
Isthmus	scarce	legislature
claim	inflation	ratify
Sutter's Mill	hydraulic mining	compromise

Lesson 1   In 1848, gold was discovered at _____.

This discovery set off a _____. In a short time,

about 90,000 fortune seekers traveled to California to find gold. Cities

such as San Francisco grew quickly. At the time, there were three main

routes to California from the United States. The fastest route took travel-

ers across the_____ of Panama. This land connects

North America and South America. The fortune seekers were known as

_____. The nickname came from the year in which

many of them came to California. One of the first things gold seekers did in

California was to stake a _____. Once that was done, the

search for gold began!

CALIFORNIA STANDARDS HSS 4.3, 4.3.2, 4.3.3, 4.3.5, 4.4, 4.4.2, 4.4.4   (continued)

68 ■ Homework and Practice Book   Use after reading Chapter 6, pages 226–257.

Name _____ Date _____

Lesson 2   The dream of finding gold brought large numbers of people to

California in a short period of time. Most people looked for gold. Some

people called _____ started businesses to provide

goods and services needed by the miners. The miners who bought these

goods or services were _____. The gold rush had

a huge impact on California's economy. Goods became hard to find,

or _____. Shortages in goods and labor caused

_____. The gold rush also affected the environment.

One of the most harmful mining methods was _____.

Lesson 3   California was then ready for a new government. A

_____ was held in Monterey in 1849.

_____ wrote a constitution that created a

_____ to be elected by the people. In November of 1849,

the people of California voted to _____ the new constitu-

tion. California's new senators asked Congress to allow California to join

the United States. This set off a huge debate about whether it should join as

a free state or a slave state. A _____ was reached, and

California joined the United States on September 9, 1850.

Because California had a large population of United States citizens at

the time, it was easier to become a state. More than 150 years after California

joined the United States, people no longer come to the state of California

looking to get rich quick from gold. But they are reminded of those who did

every time they see a San Francisco 49ers football game!

Name _____ Date _____

READING SOCIAL STUDIES: COMPARE AND CONTRAST
Focus Skill Statehood for California

DIRECTIONS Complete the Venn diagram below to show that you understand how two of the methods forty-niners used to search for gold were alike and how they were different.

Topic 1

Panning

- single person
- river water, sand, and gravel scooped into pan
- water swirled around pan

Similar

_____
_____
_____
_____
_____
_____
_____
_____
_____
_____
_____
_____
_____
_____

Topic 2

Cradle

- at least two people
- two trays; top tray filled with sand, soil, and gravel
- water poured over material in top tray as cradle is rocked

© Harcourt

 CALIFORNIA STANDARDS HSS 4.4, 4.4.2

Links to the East

DIRECTIONS Read each sentence about California's links to the eastern United States. Decide whether each statement is true (*T*) or false (*F*). Rewrite each false statement to make it true.

1 _____The telegraph used electricity to send messages over wires.

_____

2 _____ The telegraph was invented by Johnny Fry.

_____

3 _____ The Overland Mail Act helped pay for mail service between the Mississippi River and San Francisco.

_____

4 _____ It took hours to send a message by telegraph.

_____

5 _____ John Butterfield started the Overland Mail Company.

_____

6 _____ The Pony Express was put out of business by the Overland Mail Act.

_____

7 _____ An Overland Mail stagecoach could carry mail and people.

_____

8 _____ With each improvement in communication, California's ties to the rest of the United States grew stronger.

_____

© Harcourt

CALIFORNIA STANDARDS HSS 4.4, 4.4.1

Name _____ Date _____

Building the Transcontinental Railroad

DIRECTIONS Imagine you are a Chinese worker on the transcontinental railroad. You are getting ready to write a letter home. Use the questions below to help organize your thoughts.

1 Which railroad company do you work for?

_____

2 What kind of work do you do? Is it dangerous?

_____

_____

3 Are there a lot of Chinese workers? About how many workers are there?

_____

_____

_____

4 How much do you earn? Is it a good wage?

_____

_____

_____

5 What is the most track that you and the other Chinese workers laid in one day?

_____

_____

© Harcourt

CALIFORNIA STANDARDS HSS 4.4, 4.4.1, 4.4.3; CS 3   *(continued)*

72 ■ **Homework and Practice Book**   Use after reading Chapter 7, Lesson 2, pages 286–292.

Name _____ Date _____

DIRECTIONS Compare and contrast travel from the East coast to the West coast before and after the transcontinental railroad was built.

1 Before the transcontinental railroad was built, it could take weeks to travel to California on the overland route. How long did the overland route take after the transcontinental railroad was finished?

_____

2 Before the railroad, overland travel was rough and dangerous. What was the journey like for railroad passengers?

_____

_____

3 How did the transcontinental railroad increase trade for California?

_____

_____

4 How do you think California changed with the coming of the railroad?

_____

_____

_____

Rails Across California

DIRECTIONS Pretend you are a traveler in 1871. Use the map to answer these questions.

Some Railroad Lines in California, 1871

1 What is the northernmost stop in California on this map?

_____

2 What is the southernmost stop in California shown on this map?

_____

3 If you were a merchant in San Francisco, would it be easier for you to send goods to Monterey by rail or by steamship? Explain.

_____

_____

_____

4 In 1871, could you travel to Crescent City by train? Why or why not?

_____

5 Imagine you have planned a trip by train from Truckee to Bear Creek. What are some of the places you will travel through?

_____

_____

_____

CALIFORNIA STANDARDS HSS 4.1, 4.1.5, 4.4, 4.4.1; CS 5   *(continued)*

74 ■ Homework and Practice Book   Use after reading Chapter 7, Lesson 3, pages 294–297.

© Harcourt

DIRECTIONS Read the following statements. Decide whether each statement describes travelers (*T*), merchants (*M*), or railroad owners (*R*).

1 _____ They could charge what they liked for railroad tickets since there was little competition.

2 _____ They lost money when the Suez Canal opened.

3 _____ They gained more than 11 million acres of land for one railroad as a result of the Pacific Railroad Act of 1862.

4 _____ Many of them didn't make the journey west because railroad tickets were very expensive.

5 _____ Some of them lost business because goods brought in from the East sometimes cost less than goods made and sold in California.

6 _____ Their railroads were nicknamed "the Octopus."

7 _____ When the transcontinental railroad was completed, they were eager to send goods from Asia to the East coast.

8 _____ Some of them had to close their businesses after the transcontinental railroad was completed.

9 _____ The railroad made the journey from the East Coast to the West Coast easier for them.

10 _____ As they grew wealthier, they bought or started the Western Pacific and California Southern railroads.

© Harcourt

Name _____ Date _____

Skills: Read a Time Zone Map

DIRECTIONS Study the time zone map below. Use the information on the map to answer the questions.

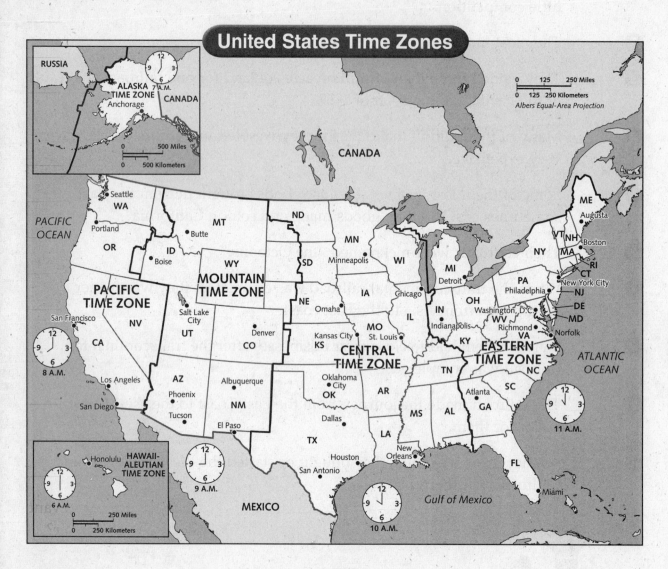

United States Time Zones

1 Which time zones would you travel through on a train trip from San Francisco to Chicago?

_____

_____

_____

CALIFORNIA STANDARDS HSS 4.1; CS 4

(continued)

76 ■ **Homework and Practice Book**   Use after reading Chapter 7, Skill Lesson, pages 298–299.

© Harcourt

2 Which time zone is Denver in? _____

3 Name two states that are in more than one time zone. _____

_____

_____

4 How many hours' difference is there between the Pacific time zone and the

Eastern time zone? _____

5 If it is 8 A.M. in New York, what time is it in Los Angeles? _____

6 If it is 6 P.M. in Chicago, what time is it in Anchorage? _____

7 If it is 3 P.M. in Honolulu, what time is it in San Francisco? _____

8 If it is 10 A.M. in Anchorage, what time is it in New York? _____

9 What is the current time where you live? Now figure out the time for each of these cities: New York, Denver, Chicago, Anchorage, and Honolulu.

_____

_____

_____

10 Imagine that you live in Detroit and your grandmother lives in Tucson. You want to call her before she leaves at 7 A.M. By what time would you need to call her?

_____

_____

© Harcourt

Name _____ Date _____

An Agricultural Power

DIRECTIONS Fill in each blank with the correct word or phrase to complete the sentence. Use the terms below.

refrigerated	canal	tenant farmers	commercial farms	Central Valley
Riverside	wheat	irrigation district	Mussel Slough	levee

1 A waterway dug across the land is a _____ canal _____.

2 Disagreements between farmers and the railroad companies led to the conflict at

_____.

3 John Bidwell's farm was located in the _____.

4 _____ are farms where crops are grown mainly to sell.

5 In 1870, orange groves were planted in the area that would soon be known as

_____.

6 The Wright Act allowed groups of farmers to form an _____.

7 A high wall made of earth which helps protect land from flooding is a

_____.

8 By 1873, California produced more _____ than any other state in the country.

9 In the late 1800s, farmers began using _____ railroad cars to send crops east.

10 _____ paid rent on their farmland with the money they earned from the sale of their crops.

CALIFORNIA STANDARDS HSS 4.4, 4.4.2, 4.4.7   *(continued)*

78 ▪ **Homework and Practice Book**   Use after reading Chapter 7, Lesson 4, pages 300–306.

© Harcourt

Name _____ Date _____

DIRECTIONS Answer the following
questions about the conflict between
the railroads and farmers.

1 In the 1870s, about how much land
did the railroad companies own in
California?

_____

_____

_____

2 What did many farmers think about
the railroad companies?

_____

_____

3 Why were the farmers at Mussel Slough angry?

_____

_____

_____

_____

4 Recall the activity "Resolve Conflict" from the previous chapter. How might
the farmers at Mussel Slough have reached a compromise with the railroad
company?

_____

_____

_____

_____

© Harcourt

Chapter 7

Name _____ Date _____

Study Guide

DIRECTIONS Martin entered a speech contest. His topic was "Historical Links to the East: Transportation and Communication." To prepare, Martin wrote out his speech to help him practice. Fill in the missing words or phrases to complete his speech. You will have to use some words twice.

Lesson 1	Lesson 2	Lesson 3	Lesson 4
communication	transcontinental	competition	commercial farms
stagecoach	railroad	Los Angeles	tenant farmers
telegraph	invest	"the Octopus"	irrigation districts
Pony Express	Central Pacific	railroads	canals
	Union Pacific		levees
	transportation		

Lesson 1   In the 1850s, _____ between California and the

eastern United States was not easy. It took months for a letter to travel

between the two coasts. On October 10, 1858, the first Overland Mail

_____ arrived in San Francisco with news from the East.

While mail delivery by stagecoach was quick, the _____ was

even quicker. The _____ lasted for less than 18

months, but it carried almost 35,000 letters during that short time. Then

the _____ replaced the Pony Express because messages

could be sent across the United States in just minutes.

CALIFORNIA STANDARDS HSS 4.4, 4.4.1, 4.4.3, 4.4.4, 4.4.7   (continued)

80 ▪ Homework and Practice Book   Use after reading Chapter 7, pages 278–307.

© Harcourt

Lesson 2   People wanted better _____

between the East and West coasts, too. Theodore Judah had

people _____ their money in a

_____. He and four others started the Central

Pacific Railroad Company. They began to build railroad tracks east from

Sacramento. Meanwhile, the Union Pacific was building a railroad west from

Council Bluffs, Iowa. Many immigrant workers were hired by both companies

to help build the railroad. The _____ hired

many workers from Ireland, and the _____

hired many workers from China. On May 10, 1869, the two railroads met in

Promontory, Utah.

Lesson 3   In time, the owners of the Central Pacific built more

_____ in California. They stretched in so many directions

that they were nicknamed _____. One of these was the

Southern Pacific, which ran from Stockton to _____. These

railroads faced little _____.

Lesson 4   Because of improved transportation, California agriculture became

a major industry. _____ met the growing demand for

food by growing crops only to sell. Some areas of California lacked water.

Farmers were able to form _____, which allowed the

farmers to build _____ to bring water to their farms.

Other areas had too much water. _____ were built to

hold back the floods. Because of the railroads, some farmers had to rent the

land they farmed and become _____.

Name _____ Date _____

READING SOCIAL STUDIES: DRAW CONCLUSIONS
🌟 Focus Skill Transportation and Communication

DIRECTIONS Complete the graphic organizers to show that you understand the importance of the growing links between California and the rest of the United States in the late 1800s. Use evidence and knowledge to draw a conclusion.

Evidence
A telegraph line linking California to the East Coast was finished in 1861.

Knowledge
Improved communication makes it easier to exchange ideas.

Conclusion
_____
_____
_____

Evidence
On May 10, 1869, the Transcontinental Railroad was finished.

Knowledge
Improved transportation makes it easier for people and goods to travel.

Conclusion
_____
_____
_____

© Harcourt

 CALIFORNIA STANDARDS HSS 4.4, 4.4.1, 4.4.3, 4.4.4

82 ▪ Homework and Practice Book   Use after reading Chapter 7, pages 278–307.

Immigration and Migration

DIRECTIONS Read each sentence about immigration and migration to California. Decide whether each statement is true (*T*) or false (*F*).

1 _____ Many of the immigrants who came to California wanted to live among people from their home countries.

2 _____ By 1900, California was home to more than 1 million people.

3 _____ During the 1870s, Chinese immigrants could hold any job they wanted.

4 _____ California Indians who went to live on reservations generally had good land and could easily grow enough food.

5 _____ Kate Douglas Wiggin set up the first free kindergarten in San Francisco in 1878.

6 _____ Immigrants who entered the United States on the Pacific coast were held on Ellis Island.

7 _____ African Americans built their own town, called Anaheim.

8 _____ Prejudice is the unfair feeling of hate or dislike for members of a certain group, race, or religion.

9 _____ Many German, French, and Italian immigrants planted vineyards.

10 _____ People from other parts of the United States came to California to build new lives during the late 1800s and early 1900s.

© Harcourt

CALIFORNIA STANDARDS HSS 4.4, 4.4.3, 4.4.4   *(continued)*

Name _____ Date _____

DIRECTIONS Ian just came back from a vacation in San Francisco. He gave a report to his class about one of the places he visited, the Japanese Tea Garden in Golden Gate Park. Read his report, and use the information to answer the questions below.

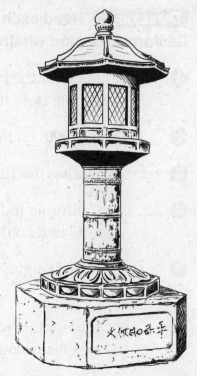

A beautiful example of Japanese culture in California is the Japanese Tea Garden. It is located in San Francisco's Golden Gate Park. The idea for the garden was a result of the 1894 World's Fair. Makoto Hagiwara, a Japanese immigrant, wanted to share his culture with his new country. The Tea Garden was the first Japanese garden in the United States. It became a permanent part of Golden Gate Park.

In the Japanese culture, a garden is considered to be one of the highest art forms. The Tea Garden includes many plants that are native to Japan. Another special feature is the 9,000-pound Lantern of Peace. The children of Japan contributed money to buy the lantern and gave it to the garden.

1 In which park is the Japanese Tea Garden?

_____

2 Why was the Japanese Tea Garden built?

_____

3 In Japan, why is a garden considered to be important?

_____

4 What kind of plants are found in the garden?

_____

5 Who helped buy the Lantern of Peace?

_____

© Harcourt

Name _____ Date _____

Southern California Grows

DIRECTIONS Read the fictional newspaper article below, about the late 1880s. Fill in the blanks to complete the article. Use the terms below to help you.

dust clouds	harbor
petroleum	reservoirs
climate	Owens Valley
ranching	derrick
population	aqueduct

Population Is Booming in Southern California!

Los Angeles—People are coming to California by the thousands! The

_____ here grew from about 11,000 people in 1880 to more than 300,000

people in 1910. Low fares on railroad tickets are luring many people into traveling

west. Some people are hoping California's warm _____ will make them

healthier. To help get supplies to all of these people, a _____ was built in

San Pedro Bay to help get supplies to Los Angeles.

San Pedro Bay

© Harcourt

CALIFORNIA STANDARDS HSS 4.4, 4.4.4, 4.4.7   *(continued)*

Another reason for this population growth is the discovery of oil, or

_____ . After the railroads found that oil was cheaper and cleaner to burn than coal, there has been a great demand for it. Some people have even tried to drill for oil in their yards. These people each

have a tower, or _____ , in their yards!

All of this growth has caused a huge strain on southern California's water supply. Water from the Los Angeles River and from human-made

lakes, or _____ , has not been enough. To solve the water problem, a large system of pipes and canals called an

_____ is bringing water to southern California from the Owens River.

Los Angeles Aqueduct

Los Angeles's need for water has upset the people living in the _____. They did not know that Los Angeles bought most of the land on both sides of the Owens River. Since Los Angeles controls the water supply, there may not be enough water in the valley for people's crops and animals. Some of the people in the valley are trying to fight back. One group used dynamite to blast a hole in the aqueduct. But the hole was fixed, and water continues to flow to Los Angeles.

Someday, pipes may bring water back to the valley. If water is returned to the

valley's dry lake bed, it will reduce the _____ . There may finally be

enough water for farming and _____ there. In the future, maybe the people of Los Angeles and of the valley will share the water they both need.

© Harcourt

Changes in Northern California

DIRECTIONS For each sentence, circle the word or phrase that makes it correct.

1 A terrible earthquake hit San Francisco in 1906 / 1908.

2 Damage from this earthquake totaled almost $100 million / $500 million.

3 After the earthquake, Amadeo Pietro Giannini helped people by giving out loans of money / food.

4 It took fewer than five / ten years for San Francisco to be rebuilt after the earthquake.

5 The population of Oakland more than doubled / tripled between 1900 and 1910.

6 Japanese immigrants moved to Sacramento to work on vegetable farms / fruit farms.

7 The Japanese community of Florin was known as the Raspberry Capital / Strawberry Capital of California.

8 In 1909, the California government built a highway system / a railroad system that made it easier for people to travel.

9 In 1914, San Francisco's leaders wanted to build a bridge / a dam on the Tuolumne River to help relieve the water shortage.

10 John Muir fought to protect the Hetch Hetchy Valley from being burned down / flooded.

© Harcourt

CALIFORNIA STANDARDS HSS 4.4, 4.4.4, 4.4.7

Skills: Read a Double-Bar Graph

DIRECTIONS Study the double-bar graphs, which show the populations of Los Angeles and San Diego and of San Francisco and Sacramento between the years 1870 and 1910. Use the graphs to answer the questions on the next page.

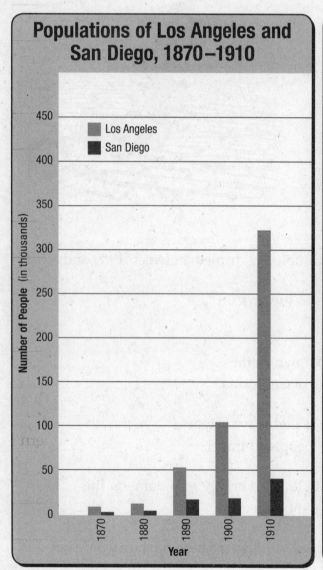

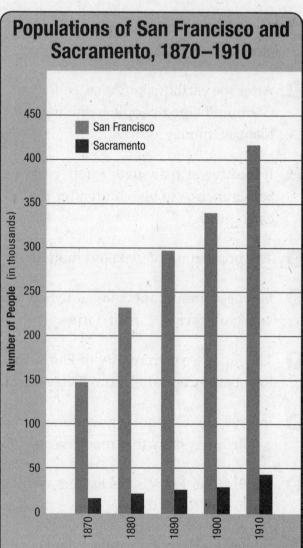

CALIFORNIA STANDARDS HSS 4.4, 4.4.4

(continued)

© Harcourt

1 Which city had a larger population in 1870, Los Angeles or San Diego?

_____

_____

2 About how many more people lived in San Francisco than in Sacramento in 1900?

_____

_____

3 Did Los Angeles or San Diego grow more between 1880 and 1890?

_____

_____

4 What years saw the greatest increase in population for all the cities?

_____

_____

5 Study the population data of each city between 1870 and 1910. Overall, did the northern cities or the southern cities have the larger total population?

_____

_____

6 Study the population data between 1870 and 1910. Look at how fast the cities' populations grew over the years. Overall, did the northern cities or the southern cities show greater population growth?

_____

_____

© Harcourt

Chapter 8

Name _____   Date _____

Study Guide

DIRECTIONS Paul wrote a short story for school about people moving to California. He wanted his story to tell how California's population growth changed the state. Fill in the missing words in Paul's short story. Use the terms below to help you.

Lesson 1	Lesson 2	Lesson 3
immigration	petroleum	Tuolumne River
migration	boom	naturalist
prejudice	derrick	Florin
reservation	aqueduct	Hetch Hetchy Valley
climate	hydroelectric power	highway

Lesson 1   In 1872, a family from China moved to San Francisco. The

family members wanted a better life for themselves. They were not alone.

In the late 1800s and early 1900s, _____ to the United

States increased a lot. People from countries such as Germany, Japan,

Armenia, and Denmark settled all over California. At the same time,

_____ also increased, because people already living

in the United States moved to California. Many people who moved to

California hoped that the mild _____ would make them

healthier. Unfortunately, the new family from China was not treated fairly.

It faced discrimination that grew out of _____ . African

Americans and Indians were not treated well either. The government even

tried to force Indians to move to an area of land set aside for them called a

_____ .

CALIFORNIA STANDARDS HSS 4.4, 4.4.3, 4.4.4, 4.4.7   *(continued)*

90 ▪ Homework and Practice Book   Use after reading Chapter 8, pages 314–337.

© Harcourt

Lesson 2   A family from Texas also moved to California. This family

lived near Los Angeles. The father found work drilling for oil, or

_____ . He worked on a _____

that held a drilling machine. The discovery of oil started a time of fast

economic growth, or _____ , in southern California.

Soon after the family moved, other relatives also moved to California. They

were looking for jobs. An uncle got a job in the Mojave Desert. He helped

build an _____ that would bring water to Los Angeles.

The moving water was used to make electricity. Electricity made by using

moving water is called _____ .

Lesson 3   In 1905, a family from Japan settled near Sacramento. The family

lived in a Japanese American community named _____ .

There the family grew strawberries. In 1909, the family went to visit friends

in San Francisco. The trip was very easy because the government had just

built a _____ system. In 1914, the son met John Muir, a

well-known _____ . Muir worked to prevent the building

of a dam on the _____ . Building it would flood a part of

Yosemite National Park called _____ . Although people

didn't want to damage a national park, the dam was built anyway. San

Francisco got its water, but the plan made many people angry.

Name _____ Date _____

READING SOCIAL STUDIES: DRAW CONCLUSIONS

⭐Focus Skill A Growing Economy

DIRECTIONS Complete the graphic organizers to show that you understand how to use evidence and knowledge to draw conclusions about the growth of California's economy.

Evidence

California was seen by many immigrants as a land of opportunity.

Knowledge

People from different cultures can learn from each other's ways of life and traditions.

Conclusion

_____

_____

_____

Evidence

Oil was discovered in California in the late 1800s.

Knowledge

The demand for oil increased because it is used to fuel automobiles and railroad locomotives.

Conclusion

_____

_____

_____

© Harcourt

 CALIFORNIA STANDARDS HSS 4.4, 4.4.3, 4.4.6

Use after reading Chapter 8, pages 314–337.

Into a New Century

DIRECTIONS Fill in the blanks to complete the sentences about California in the early 1900s. Use the terms below.

cotton	films	Panama Canal
bribe	consumer goods	suffrage
talkies	World War I	airplane factory
aviation	amendments	car

1 To _____ someone is to promise or give the person money or a gift to get him or her to do something.

2 Changes to a constitution are called _____ .

3 Glenn Martin built California's first _____ in 1909.

4 In 1911, women in California gained the right to vote, or _____ .

5 In the early 1900s, many theater owners replaced live actors with

_____ .

6 In 1914, the _____ opened, which helped increase trade between California and the rest of the world.

7 In 1917, the United States entered _____ after Germany began attacking United States ships.

8 During World War I, California supplied _____ for uniforms.

9 The making and flying of airplanes is called _____ .

10 In the late 1920s, motion pictures with sound were called _____ .

11 By 1925, there was one _____ for every three people in Los Angeles.

12 Products made for people to use are called _____ .

© Harcourt

CALIFORNIA STANDARDS HSS 4.4, 4.4.6, 4.4.9, 4.5, 4.5.4

(continued)

Name _____ Date _____

DIRECTIONS Read the statements below. Identify the person who might have said each one. Write Glenn Martin, Caroline Severance, Hiram Johnson, or Louis B. Mayer.

1 "I was a moviemaker who started in business by owning one movie theater in 1907.

I am _____."

2 "I was the first woman in California to register to vote.

I am _____."

3 "I was a pioneer in California's aviation industry.

I am _____."

4 "I helped reform the government of California.

I am _____."

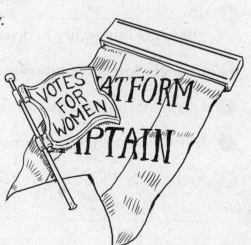

5 "I built an airplane factory in Santa Ana.

I am _____."

6 "I was one of the first successful moviemakers.

I am _____."

7 "I was elected governor of California.

I am _____."

8 "I was a leader in the suffrage movement.

I am _____."

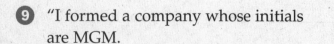

9 "I formed a company whose initials are MGM.

I am _____."

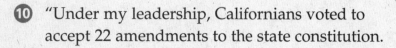

10 "Under my leadership, Californians voted to accept 22 amendments to the state constitution.

I am _____."

© Harcourt

Hard Times for Californians

DIRECTIONS Circle the word or phrase that makes each sentence correct.

1 Most migrant workers were paid well / poorly.

2 The Great Depression was a time when people had little money and unemployment was low / high.

3 After the dust storms, many people from the Dust Bowl moved to California / New York, but many could not find steady jobs.

4 The area of the United States affected by floods / drought in the early 1930s was known as the Dust Bowl.

5 It took four / six years to complete the Golden Gate Bridge.

6 A stock market crash led to the Great Depression / Dust Bowl.

7 The Central Valley Project helped control floods / dust storms.

8 President Roosevelt promised Americans a "new deal" / a "real deal."

9 Dorothea Lange's photographs helped to / did not help to persuade the government to help farmworkers.

10 John Steinbeck's book *The Grapes of Wrath* told of the unfair ways that migrant workers were treated in the San Joaquin Valley / Dust Bowl.

11 Projects such as the Golden Gate Bridge hurt / helped workers in California.

12 In October 1929, stock prices fell so low that the drop was called a freefall / crash.

CALIFORNIA STANDARDS HSS 4.4, 4.4.5, 4.4.9

(continued)

Name _____ Date _____

DIRECTIONS Use the paragraph below to answer questions about the life of author John Steinbeck.

John Steinbeck was born in Salinas in 1902. When he was a teenager, he decided to become a writer. In 1919, Steinbeck entered Stanford University. He left Stanford in 1925.

Critics believe that Steinbeck wrote most of his best fiction during the 1930s. During this time, he often worked closely with migrant workers. He started to understand their problems. His best-known book, *The Grapes of Wrath*, focused on the lives and problems of migrant workers. This novel won a Pulitzer Prize and a National Book Award.

John Steinbeck

During World War II, Steinbeck did patriotic writing and served as a war correspondent. After the war, Steinbeck continued to write. In 1962, John Steinbeck was awarded the Nobel Prize in Literature. He died six years later in 1968.

1 When did John Steinbeck decide to become a writer?

_____

_____

2 When did Steinbeck write most of his best fiction?

_____

3 What is the title of Steinbeck's best-known book?

_____

4 What did Steinbeck do during World War II?

_____

5 Which prize did Steinbeck win in 1962?

_____

© Harcourt

Skills: Make a Thoughtful Decision

DIRECTIONS Read the steps for making a thoughtful decision. The steps are out of order. Write the steps in their correct order.

- Think about possible consequences of each choice. Decide which choice will have the best consequences.

- Make a list of choices to help you reach your goal.

- Put your decision into action.

- Gather the information you will need to make a good decision.

1

↓

2

↓

3

↓

4

© Harcourt

CALIFORNIA STANDARDS HSS 4.4, 4.4.5

(continued)

Name _____ Date _____

DIRECTIONS Review some decisions that were made during the Great Depression. Then answer the questions.

1. Superintendent Leo Hart decided to build Weedpatch School. What are two other choices he could have made?

_____

_____

_____

_____

2. What are some consequences of building Weedpatch School?

_____

_____

_____

3. The Golden Gate Bridge is a very visible result of a decision. What was the goal of building the Golden Gate Bridge?

_____

_____

4. President Roosevelt and Congress created the New Deal programs. What was the goal of these programs?

_____

_____

5. What are other choices that the President and Congress could have made about the New Deal and its programs?

_____

_____

Name _____ Date _____

California and World War II

DIRECTIONS Study the poster from World War II. Then answer the questions.

When the United States entered World War II in 1941, huge numbers of people went into the armed forces. Workers were needed to replace those who had gone off to war. Most people, especially women, went to work in factories, steel mills, shipyards, and offices to support the war effort.

Californians at home played an important role during World War II. New military bases were built in California to prepare soldiers for fighting. People realized that food rationing was necessary to make sure that the members of the armed forces would have enough to eat. Children helped by collecting metal, rubber, and paper to be recycled.

1 What is this poster about? _____

_____

2 Why were posters like this one made? _____

_____

_____

3 Why was this message important? _____

_____

_____

4 What details in the poster got the message across? _____

_____

_____

 CALIFORNIA STANDARDS HSS 4.4, 4.4.5   *(continued)*

Name _____ Date _____

Describe the effect of World War II on
the group of Californians mentioned in each question.

1 What was the effect of the war on Japanese
Americans?

_____

_____

_____

_____

_____

**World War II patch for
the 442nd Regimental
Combat Team**

2 What was the effect of the war on African Americans?

_____

_____

_____

3 What was the effect of the war on skilled Mexican farmworkers?

_____

_____

_____

4 What was the effect of the war on women?

_____

_____

_____

_____

Chapter 9

Study Guide

DIRECTIONS At a family reunion, you listen to your great-grandmother tell stories about life during the Great Depression and World War II. Later, you decide to find out more about these events to include in a family history book. Fill in the blanks to complete the sentences using words from the lists below.

Lesson 1	Lesson 2	Lesson 3
bribes	stocks	munitions
reform	depression	shortage
suffrage	unemployment	braceros
amendments	migrant workers	recycle
aviation	Dust Bowl	relocation camps

Lesson 1 In the early 1900s, California was an exciting place.

Under Governor Hiram Johnson, Californians voted to accept 22

_____ to the state constitution. These changes helped

_____ the state government. Big businesses could no

longer get their way by offering _____ to officials. Women

gained _____, or the right to vote, in state elections. The

opening of the Panama Canal meant shipping routes between the East coast

and California were much shorter. After World War I, the economy was

strong. New industries, such as the airplane, or _____,

industry, came to California. Also, new products were being made. People

could afford to buy things such as vacuum cleaners and cars. Movies

also started to become popular. Hollywood became the movie capital of

the world!

© Harcourt

CALIFORNIA STANDARDS HSS 4.4, 4.4.4, 4.4.5, 4.4.6   *(continued)*

Lesson 2   The 1930s brought a bad _____. It began when

shares of ownership in a company, called _____, lost value

in 1929. People had less money, so they bought fewer goods. Businesses

began to fail. Then, outside of California, a drought began. The central part

of the United States became known as the _____. The

drought caused many families in those states to want to leave. Some fami-

lies wanted to come to California. But many of these farmers could not find

steady work in California. Instead, they moved wherever the crops were

and became known as _____. Many Californians wanted

to keep these workers out because _____ was high. They

didn't want other people taking jobs away from Californians.

Lesson 3   The United States entered World War II in 1941. After the Japanese

attacked Pearl Harbor, people became afraid. Japanese Americans were

ordered to move to _____. During the war, factories made

war supplies. Because of a _____ of local workers, people

came to California to work. Some new workers had jobs in factories making

military supplies and weapons, or _____. Skilled

farmworkers from Mexico, or _____, did farm labor

during the war. Women worked in factories. Even children helped out with

the war. They collected materials for the military to _____.

By the time the war ended in 1945, life had changed a lot for Californians!

© Harcourt

Name _____ Date _____

READING SOCIAL STUDIES: CAUSE AND EFFECT

(Focus Skill) Growing and Changing

DIRECTIONS Complete the graphic organizers below to show that you understand the causes and effects of change and growth in California from the early 1900s through World War II.

Cause

The stock market crashes on October 29, 1929.

→ **Effect**

_____
_____
_____
_____
_____
_____
_____
_____

Cause

The United States enters World War II in 1941.

→ **Effect**

_____
_____
_____
_____
_____
_____
_____
_____

© Harcourt

 CALIFORNIA STANDARDS HSS 4.4, 4.4.5; HI 3

Name _____ Date _____

Changes After World War II

DIRECTIONS Many industries became important to California's economy after World War II. Think about each of the California industries listed in the boxes. Write an X next to each effect caused by the industry.

Automobile Industry

1 _____ Road traffic increased.

2 _____ Most people moved closer to their jobs.

3 _____ Freeways were built.

4 _____ Suburbs grew.

5 _____ It became impossible for workers to commute.

Computer Industry

6 _____ Fewer high-tech electronic companies opened.

7 _____ The silicon chip was invented.

8 _____ Computers became less expensive.

9 _____ Space travel became possible.

10 _____ Computers became smaller and faster.

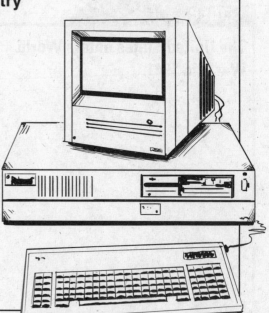

© Harcourt

 CALIFORNIA STANDARDS HSS 4.4, 4.4.5, 4.4.6; HI 3   *(continued)*

Aerospace Industry

11 _____ It helped develop more advanced rocket engines.

12 _____ It helped reduce traffic on freeways.

13 _____ It put jet engines in most cars.

14 _____ It improved air travel.

15 _____ It helped Americans land on the moon.

DIRECTIONS Choose a job in one of the industries, and plan a brief job advertisement for it. Write four sentences giving reasons why it is an exciting job to have in California.

Help Wanted!

Advertisement title: _____

Work in the _____ industry!

Reason 1: _____

_____

Reason 2: _____

_____

Reason 3: _____

_____

Reason 4: _____

_____

It's great to work in California!

© Harcourt

Skills: Read a Road Map

DIRECTIONS Study the map of the San Francisco Bay area shown below. Use the map to answer the questions on the next page.

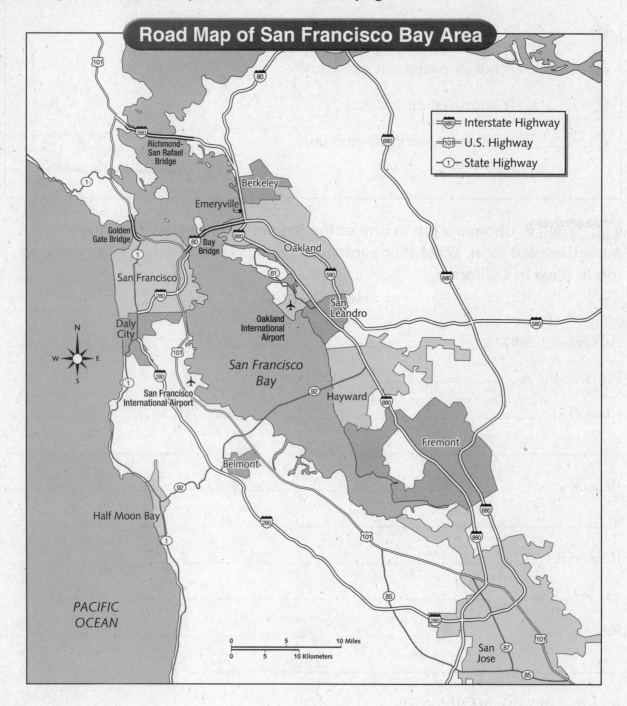

Road Map of San Francisco Bay Area

CALIFORNIA STANDARDS CS 4   *(continued)*

106 ■ **Homework and Practice Book**   Use after reading Chapter 10, Skill Lesson, pages 398–399.

© Harcourt

Name _____ Date _____

1 Which highway runs by San Francisco International Airport?

_____

2 Which highway shown on the map is closest to Oakland International Airport?

_____

3 About how many miles is it from Daly City to Belmont on Interstate 280?

_____

4 The Bay Bridge is part of what Interstate Highway?

_____

5 Which highway would you take to get from Belmont to Hayward?

_____

6 Which roads would you take to get from the San Jose area to the San Leandro area if you were heading east on State Highway 85?

_____

_____

7 How would you get from Emeryville to Half Moon Bay?

_____

_____

8 How would you get from Half Moon Bay to San Jose?

_____

_____

_____

Rights for All Californians

DIRECTIONS Read the following information about *Mendez v. Westminster* and its effect on schools. Then organize the information on the time line on the next page.

In 1896, the United States Supreme Court ruled in favor of a law that allowed segregation in public places if facilities were "separate but equal." The rule said that it was all right to have separate railroad cars for African Americans. The only restriction was that the railroad cars had to be similar to those for white people. This idea of "separate but equal" was then applied to all aspects of life, including schools. African Americans were not the only group affected by this rule. Mexican Americans and other groups also faced the idea of "separate but equal." Many people felt that this segregation was a form of discrimination.

Gonzalo Mendez and four other Mexican American fathers decided to fight the ruling. They thought children of Mexican and Latin descent should not have to go to a separate school. In March 1945, they filed a claim in the federal court in Los Angeles. The case became known as *Mendez v. Westminster*.

In February 1946, Judge Paul J. McCormick ruled that Mendez and the other fathers were correct. In June 1947, California Governor Earl Warren signed a new law passed by the California legislature. The new law said that the "separate but equal" ruling could no longer be applied to California schools.

Mendez v. Westminster also affected African Americans. In February 1951, the parents of 20 African American schoolchildren in Topeka, Kansas, filed a lawsuit to stop segregation in schools there. This case was called *Brown v. Board of Education of Topeka*. Their lawsuit was eventually heard by the United States Supreme Court. The parents argued that separate schools made the children feel as though they were not equal to their peers. This was the same argument used in *Mendez v. Westminster*. In May 1954, all of the Supreme Court justices decided the parents were correct. The Court said that the idea of "separate but equal" broke the Fourteenth Amendment to the Constitution. This amendment says that all citizens must be treated equally. The court said that segregation in all schools must end. Soon other states began to join California in saying that "separate but equal" schools were illegal.

© Harcourt

CALIFORNIA STANDARDS HSS 4.4, 4.4.8; CS 1

(continued)

Name _____ Date _____

- California Governor Earl Warren signs a law that says the "separate but equal" ruling can no longer be applied to California schools.

- The Supreme Court rules that "separate but equal" schools are against the Fourteenth Amendment.

- *Brown v. Board of Education of Topeka* is brought to court.

- Gonzalo Mendez and four other Mexican American fathers file a claim in a case called *Mendez v. Westminster*.

- Judge Paul J. McCormick rules that Mendez and the other fathers are correct.

© Harcourt

A Diverse State

DIRECTIONS For each sentence, circle the word or phrase that makes it correct.

1. All people born in the United States are citizens / immigrants of the United States.

2. The diverse cultures of immigrants have made California multicultural / unicultural.

3. Culture includes language, food, and religious beliefs / classes you take in school.

4. The Punjabi American Festival celebrates the heritage of people from Cambodia / India.

5. Many Punjabis are members of the Jewish / Sikh religion.

6. Cinco de Mayo celebrates Mexican / Vietnamese heritage.

7. The Celtic Celebration celebrates the heritage of people from Scotland, Wales, and Ireland / Laos.

8. In Los Angeles, the Watts Towers Day of the Violin / Drum focuses on one musical instrument.

9. Citizenship Day is celebrated on July 4 / September 17.

10. The government has passed laws to make it harder for / easier for illegal immigrants to stay in the United States.

© Harcourt

CALIFORNIA STANDARDS HSS 4.4, 4.4.4 *(continued)*

110 ▪ **Homework and Practice Book** Use after reading Chapter 10, Lesson 3, pages 406–409.

Name _____ Date _____

DIRECTIONS Use the information below to
complete the sentences or answer the questions.

Chinese moon cakes

When Chinese immigrants came to California
during the gold rush, they brought many of their
traditions with them. One of those traditions is the
Mid-Autumn Festival, or Moon Festival. The festival
is more than 1,000 years old. Asian communities all
over the world celebrate the festival. Although the festival date changes each year,
it is always held in the fall during a full moon. In Chinese culture, the full moon is a
symbol of coming together.

The Mid-Autumn Festival celebrates the harvest season and is a time for families
to gather together. During the festival, families return to their parents' homes for a
large meal. One special food that is eaten during this celebration is the moon cake.
Moon cakes are small round pastries with a flaky golden crust. They are baked with
sweet fillings of nuts, mashed red beans, lotus-seed paste, or Chinese dates. The
moon cakes are given as gifts.

People who can't go home are still able to celebrate the Mid-Autumn Festival.
They can go outdoors, look up at the full moon, and think of their families.

1 Another name for the Mid-Autumn Festival is the _____ .

2 The Mid-Autumn Festival is more than _____ years old.

3 What are moon cakes?

_____

_____

4 If people can't be with their families during the festival, what can they do?

_____

_____

5 How do you think the Mid-Autumn Festival is similar to Thanksgiving?

_____

_____

Chapter 10

Study Guide

DIRECTIONS Fill in the missing words for Janelle's presentation for Citizenship Day. Use the terms below to help you complete the presentation.

Lesson 1		Lesson 2	Lesson 3
technology	silicon chip	boycott	multicultural
freeway	aerospace	segregation	ethnic group
commute	diverse	civil rights	heritage
urban sprawl	Fremont	labor union	culture
high-tech	Pasadena	strike	festivals

Lesson 1   After World War II, industries such as the automobile industry and the electronics industry grew. One automobile factory in _____ built 5 million vehicles! New industries led to the construction of whole communities away from urban centers, causing _____. Workers could travel to work, or _____, on a divided highway called a _____. California's economy became more _____ with so many new industries growing quickly. To support the new computer and aviation industries, more than 200 _____ electronic companies opened in the San Francisco area alone. Computer _____ helped make it possible for people to land on the moon. The Jet Propulsion Laboratory in _____ became a leader in the _____ industry. The invention of the _____ helped the computer industry.

CALIFORNIA STANDARDS HSS 4.4, 4.4.4, 4.4.5, 4.4.6, 4.4.8   *(continued)*

112 ▪ **Homework and Practice Book**   Use after reading Chapter 10, pages 392–409.

© Harcourt

Lesson 2   Californians from many different backgrounds have worked

hard to protect what the United States Constitution promises—people's

_____ . The parents of Sylvia Mendez were upset that their

daughter had to go to a separate school. They fought and won the case

against school _____ . Cesar Chavez and Dolores Huerta

wanted to help migrant farmworkers. They organized farmworkers to form

a _____ . Chavez encouraged workers to stop doing their jobs

if an employer was unfair. He led grape pickers in a _____ .

Then he encouraged people to _____ grapes until the problem

was fixed. Other people have continued to fight for equality.

Lesson 3   Californians come from all over the world. The members

of each _____ have brought the ways of their former

country with them to share in their new country. These ways, such as

a common language, food, and religious beliefs, make up the group's

_____ . When the ways of life are handed down for genera-

tions, they make up a group's _____ . Immigrants help make

California a _____ state. Many California cities have cultural

_____ , or celebrations, each year. These help make California

a special place to live.

© Harcourt

READING SOCIAL STUDIES: CAUSE AND EFFECT

(Focus Skill) Into Modern Times

DIRECTIONS Complete the graphic organizer below to show that you understand the causes and effects of key events that helped shape California in the half century after World War II.

Cause		Effect
Workers who come to California during the war decide to stay.	→	_____

Cause		Effect
Some groups in California face discrimination.	→	_____

CALIFORNIA STANDARDS HSS 4.4, 4.4.4, 4.4.6, 4.4.8

114 ■ Homework and Practice Book   Use after reading Chapter 10, pages 392–409.

© Harcourt

Name _____ Date _____

A Modern Economy

DIRECTIONS Use the table to answer the questions below.

California's Top Ten Agricultural Export Markets, 2002			
Rank	Country/Region	Value of Principal Exports (in millions)	Leading Exports
1	Canada	$1,199	lettuce, processed tomatoes, table grapes
2	European Union	$1,128	almonds, wine, walnuts
3	Japan	$905	rice, almonds, hay
4	China/Hong Kong	$345	table grapes, oranges, cotton
5	Mexico	$293	dairy, table grapes, processed tomatoes
6	Korea	$274	oranges, beef, cotton
7	Taiwan	$212	cotton, peaches and nectarines, rice
8	Indonesia	$101	cotton, table grapes, dairy
9	India	$94	almonds, cotton, table grapes
10	Malaysia	$60	table grapes, oranges, almonds

Source: California Department of Food and Agriculture

1 What are California's leading exports to China/Hong Kong?

_____

2 What are California's leading exports to Taiwan?

_____

3 What was the value of exports to Japan in 2002?

_____

4 How many of the top ten markets receive California almonds?

_____

5 To which countries/regions does California export cotton?

_____

 CALIFORNIA STANDARDS HSS 4.4, 4.4.6

Use after reading Chapter 11, Lesson 1, pages 430–435.

© Harcourt

Skills: Read a Land Use and Products Map

DIRECTIONS Use the products map of California to answer the questions on the next page.

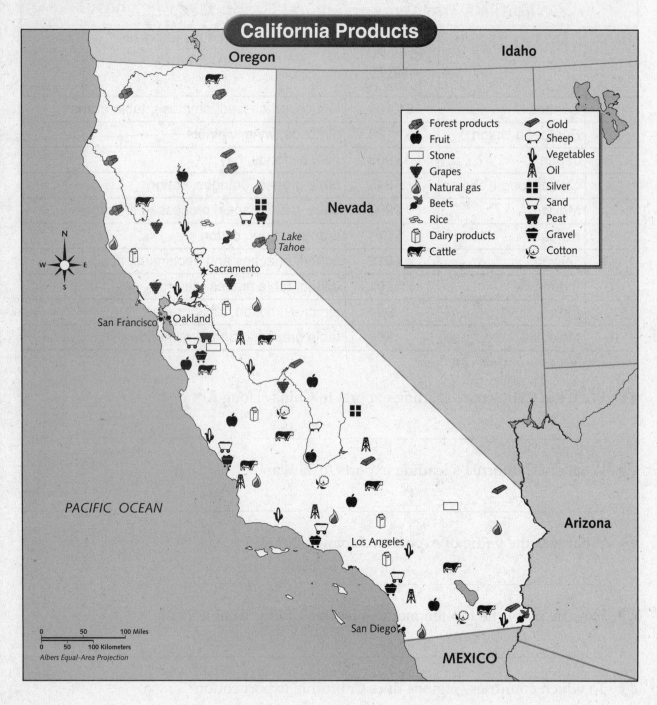

California Products

Oregon

Idaho

Nevada

Lake Tahoe

★ Sacramento

San Francisco • Oakland

Arizona

PACIFIC OCEAN

Los Angeles

0   50   100 Miles
0   50   100 Kilometers
Albers Equal-Area Projection

San Diego

MEXICO

Legend:

- Forest products
- Fruit
- Stone
- Grapes
- Natural gas
- Beets
- Rice
- Dairy products
- Cattle
- Gold
- Sheep
- Vegetables
- Oil
- Silver
- Sand
- Peat
- Gravel
- Cotton

© Harcourt

CALIFORNIA STANDARDS HSS 4.4, 4.4.6; CS 4   *(continued)*

116 ■ Homework and Practice Book   Use after reading Chapter 11, Skill Lesson, pages 436–437.

1 How does a products map show various products?

_____

2 What is the symbol for dairy products?

_____

3 What is the symbol for natural gas?

_____

4 Peat is a kind of earth made of soil, water, and grass. Where in California is most peat found?

_____

5 What kind of farm animal is raised in large numbers in the land to the north of Sacramento?

_____

6 What kind of fuel would you find south of Los Angeles?

_____

7 In what part of the state are most forest products found?

_____

8 What five products would you find closest to the border of California and Mexico?

_____

_____

9 In which part of the state are most food products grown?

_____

10 What products can be found within 50 miles of Lake Tahoe?

_____

_____

© Harcourt

A State of the Arts

DIRECTIONS Read the paragraphs below. Use the information to answer the questions on the next page.

Walt Disney is one of the most famous names in the history of animation. He was the first person to add sound to his animated short films. He was also the first person to produce a feature-length animated movie.

Most of the best-known films from the Disney Studio were made using cel animation. The term *cel* comes from the word celluloid (SEL•yuh•loyd). Celluloid was the material first used for animation. Cel animation requires several artists. A layout artist decides what backgrounds are needed and how each character will look and act. A background artist draws the backgrounds for a film. Artists called animators create the drawings of the characters. Each drawing is slightly different from the one before. When the drawings are shown in order very fast, the character looks as if it can move just like a real person or animal.

Next, a group of artists must trace the drawings onto cels, or clear sheets of film. The cels and backgrounds are put in order. Then, the cels are photographed frame by frame over the correct background. A soundtrack with music and real voices talking for the characters is added last. Finally, the movie is ready to be seen.

Today, much of the animation is done using computers. Although computers can speed things up, the process still takes a long time. One large computer system may take about 6 hours to make one frame. During the movie, one frame lasts for only $\frac{1}{24}$ of a second on the screen. Some frames take as long as 90 hours to complete!

Animated movies can be great fun to watch, because they are not limited by the real world. However, both cel animators and animators who use computers know that it takes months to create just a few hours of movie magic.

© Harcourt

CALIFORNIA STANDARDS HSS 4.4, 4.4.9

(continued)

118 ▪ **Homework and Practice Book**   Use after reading Chapter 11, Lesson 2, pages 438–442.

Name _____ Date _____

① What California filmmaker produced the first feature-length animated movie?

_____

② What kind of animation did the Disney Studio use to make most of its best-known films?

_____

_____

③ What kinds of artists are needed to make cel animation?

_____

_____

④ How long does it take to make one animated frame by computer?

_____

⑤ How difficult do you think it is to make a movie using animation? Explain why you think this, using reasons you learned in the reading.

_____

_____

_____

_____

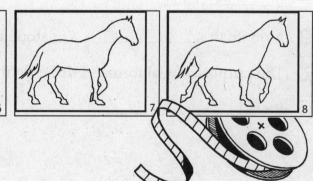

© Harcourt

Name _____   Date _____

Education in California

DIRECTIONS Fill in each blank with the correct word or phrase to complete these sentences about education in California. Use the terms below.

largest	Alta California
private schools	San Francisco
university	public schools
600,000	9,000
high school	future

1 There are nearly _____ public schools in California.

2 California's first constitution set up

a state _____ system for students to go to after high school.

3 _____ are funded in large part by city and state taxes.

4 In 1850, the first public school that was paid for by city taxes opened in

_____ .

5 _____ are mostly funded by private groups and individuals.

6 San Francisco's first public _____ opened in 1856.

7 There have been private schools in California since the time the Spanish ruled

_____ .

8 California has the _____ system of colleges and universities in the United States.

9 More than _____ students in California attend private schools.

10 The purpose of California's educational system is to prepare students for

the _____ .

© Harcourt

CALIFORNIA STANDARDS HSS 4.4, 4.4.8

Name _____ Date _____

Overcoming Challenges

DIRECTIONS Identify whether each resource is renewable (*R*) or nonrenewable (*N*).

1 _____ gold

2 _____ oil

3 _____ trees

4 _____ coal

5 _____ water

DIRECTIONS Draw a line from each term to its definition.

6 deficit   the protection and wise use of natural resources

7 pollution   the result of a state that has spent more money than it has

8 conservation   making choices based on how those choices will affect life in the future

9 energy crisis   anything that makes a natural resource dirty or unsafe to use

10 long-term planning   what occurs when there is not enough power to meet the demand for energy

© Harcourt

[**CALIFORNIA STANDARDS HSS 4.1**]

Skills: Solve a Problem

DIRECTIONS Review the steps to solving a problem. Then answer the questions below.

1 A city with a lot of traffic has a high level of air pollution. Identify the problem.

_____

2 Suppose a power shortage was caused by people using a lot of electricity. Another power outage occurred immediately after an earthquake. Are the causes of the two shortages the same? Explain.

_____

_____

3 Some shortages can be prevented through conservation. What are some advantages and disadvantages of conservation?

_____

_____

_____

4 With so many cars burning gas and oil, this nonrenewable resource is being used up quickly. What are some possible solutions to this problem?

_____

_____

5 Too many trees have been taken from an area of a forest. What could be a solution to this problem?

_____

_____

© Harcourt

CALIFORNIA STANDARDS HSS 4.1; HI 4 *(continued)*

Name _____ Date _____

1 What is the problem?

_____

_____

2 Can you identify the cause or causes of the problem? Explain.

_____

_____

3 What are some possible solutions to the problem?

_____

_____

4 What are some advantages and disadvantages of each solution?

_____

_____

_____

5 Choose the best solution. How will you put your solution into action?

_____

_____

© Harcourt

Chapter 11

Name _____ Date _____

Study Guide

DIRECTIONS You have an idea for a Chamber of Commerce brochure telling why California is known as the "Golden State." Use the terms below to fill in the missing words in this brochure.

Lesson 1	Lesson 2	Lesson 3	Lesson 4
international trade	special effects	public	long-term planning
importing	architects	private	conservation
interdependence	Los Angeles	future	renewable
food processing	San Francisco	education	nonrenewable
tourism	San Diego	constitution	deficit

Lesson 1   Welcome to the "Golden State" of California! People usually think

of California as a place to take a vacation. The _____

industry is just one of the industries that help California's economy. The _____

agriculture industry is another important industry. _____

is an important part of this industry. Trade relationships create

_____ between California and people in other places.

California does a lot of _____ (bringing in) and export-

ing (shipping out) of goods. The state's location on the Pacific Ocean makes

it ideal for _____ .

🐻 **CALIFORNIA STANDARDS HSS 4.4, 4.4.6, 4.4.8, 4.4.9**   *(continued)*

124 ■ Homework and Practice Book   Use after reading Chapter 11, pages 430–455.

© Harcourt

Name _____ Date _____

Lesson 2   California is well-known as the home of the movie industry—making fantasy seem real through the use of _____. However, moviemaking is not the only art in California! The city of _____ is home to the J. Paul Getty Center, where people can view great works of art. _____ such as Julia Morgan have left their mark in the great buildings they have designed. The Centro Cultural de la Raza in _____, the Asian Art Museum in _____, and the California State Indian Museum in Sacramento all showcase the work of great artists.

Lesson 3   None of California's contributions would have been possible without _____. California's first _____ set up public schools. Delegate Robert Semple knew the importance of a good education in preparing students for the _____. Both _____ schools (funded by taxes) and _____ schools (funded by groups and individuals) help educate the people of California.

Lesson 4   Californians face many challenges, especially energy shortages. _____ can help prevent a shortage, or _____, of resources. This is true for resources that are _____ (able to be made again quickly) and _____ (not able to be made again quickly). Practicing _____ is another way that Californians protect resources while making valuable contributions to society.

© Harcourt

Name _____ Date _____

READING SOCIAL STUDIES: SUMMARIZE
⭐Focus Skill The Golden State

DIRECTIONS Complete the graphic organizers to show that you understand
how to summarize about industries, activities, and institutions in California.

Key Fact

California has a powerful economy supported by international trade and the agriculture, high tech, and service industries.

Key Fact

California's educational system prepares students for the future.

Summary

_____
_____
_____
_____
_____
_____

Key Fact

Californians face energy shortages.

Key Fact

Californians are researching ways to use renewable resources.

Summary

_____
_____
_____
_____

 CALIFORNIA STANDARDS HSS 4.4, 4.4.6, 4.4.8

© Harcourt

A Plan for Government

DIRECTIONS For each sentence, circle the word or phrase that makes it correct.

1 The first ten amendments to the United States Constitution are known as the Bill of Rights / Preamble.

2 Congress is the legislative / judical branch of the federal government.

3 The federal government is located in Sacramento / Washington, D.C.

4 The United States Congress makes laws for the entire nation / state of California.

5 The Cabinet is a group of the President's most important advisers / senators.

6 Supreme Court justices are appointed for 10 years / life.

7 Trade between states is managed by the federal / state government.

8 A refund / tax is money that a government collects from its citizens, usually to pay for services.

9 Both the federal and state governments are divided into two / three branches.

10 Three / Five people from California have been elected President.

11 The United States House of Representatives has 100 / 435 members.

12 The state with the most representatives in the United States House of Representatives is California / New York.

13 Only the state government / federal government has the power to declare war on another nation.

CALIFORNIA STANDARDS HSS 4.5, 4.5.1, 4.5.3

(continued)

Name _____ Date _____

1 _____ Collects property taxes on homes, businesses, and farms

2 _____ Issues driver's licenses

3 _____ Prints money

4 _____ Controls trade within the state

5 _____ Sets up post offices

6 _____ Takes care of reservoirs and canals that collect and carry water

7 _____ Passes laws that apply to the people in a particular city

8 _____ Takes care of water pipes in a specific region

9 _____ Sets up national standards to make sure air quality is good

10 _____ Collects money through sales tax

11 _____ Cares for national parks and historical sites

12 _____ Controls trade between the United States and other countries

13 _____ Makes up laws that affect only the people within California

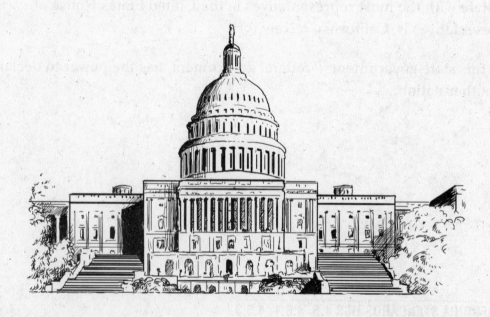

© Harcourt

Name _____ Date _____

California State Government

DIRECTIONS Compare and contrast the United States Constitution and the California Constitution. Use the phrases listed below to complete the diagram. Write each phrase in the correct area. Use each phrase only once. Remember, if a phrase is written in the part where the two circles meet, it must be true for both of the constitutions.

executive branch	referendum
Bill of Rights	written in 1787
judicial branch	highest law of the land
Declaration of Rights	recall of officials
initiatives	legislative branch

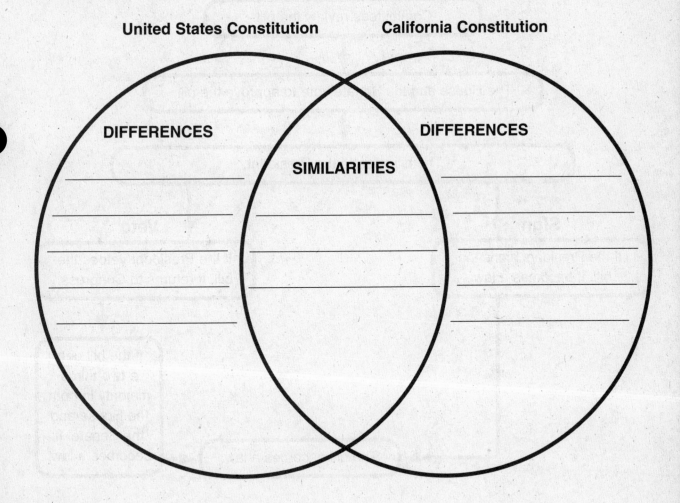

United States Constitution   California Constitution

DIFFERENCES   DIFFERENCES

SIMILARITIES

© Harcourt

Skills: Read a Flowchart

DIRECTIONS Study the flowchart below, which explains how a bill becomes a federal law. Use the flowchart to help you answer the questions on the next page.

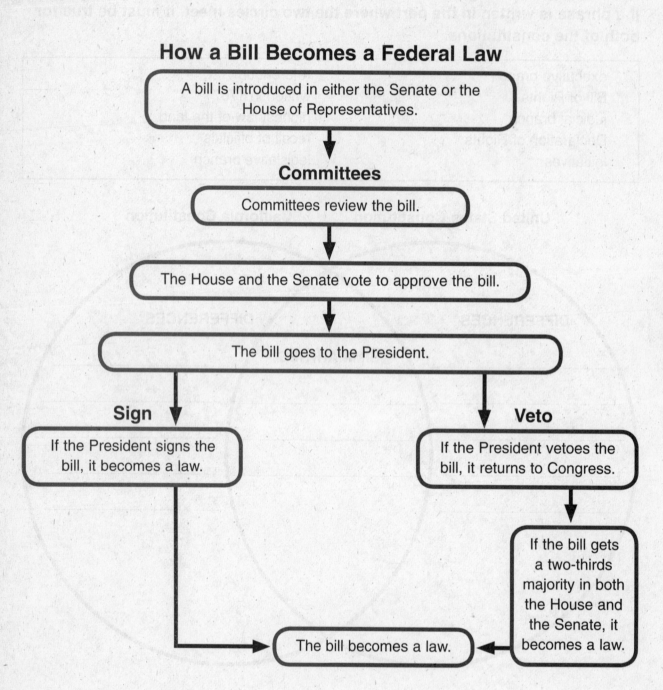

How a Bill Becomes a Federal Law

A bill is introduced in either the Senate or the House of Representatives.

Committees

Committees review the bill.

The House and the Senate vote to approve the bill.

The bill goes to the President.

Sign

If the President signs the bill, it becomes a law.

Veto

If the President vetoes the bill, it returns to Congress.

If the bill gets a two-thirds majority in both the House and the Senate, it becomes a law.

The bill becomes a law.

© Harcourt

CALIFORNIA STANDARDS HSS 4.5, 4.5.3, 4.5.4   *(continued)*

130 ■ **Homework and Practice Book**   Use after reading Chapter 12, Skill Lesson, pages 478–479.

Name _____ Date _____

1 Where is a bill introduced?

_____

_____

2 What is the next step after a bill has been introduced?

_____

_____

3 Who must vote to approve the bill before it goes to the President of the United States?

_____

_____

4 What happens if the President signs the bill?

_____

_____

5 Compare this flowchart to the one on pages 478–479 of your textbook. If either the President of the United States or the Governor of California vetoes a bill, how can it still become a law?

_____

_____

Name _____ Date _____

Local Governments

DIRECTIONS Match the form of local government with the person or group that represents it.

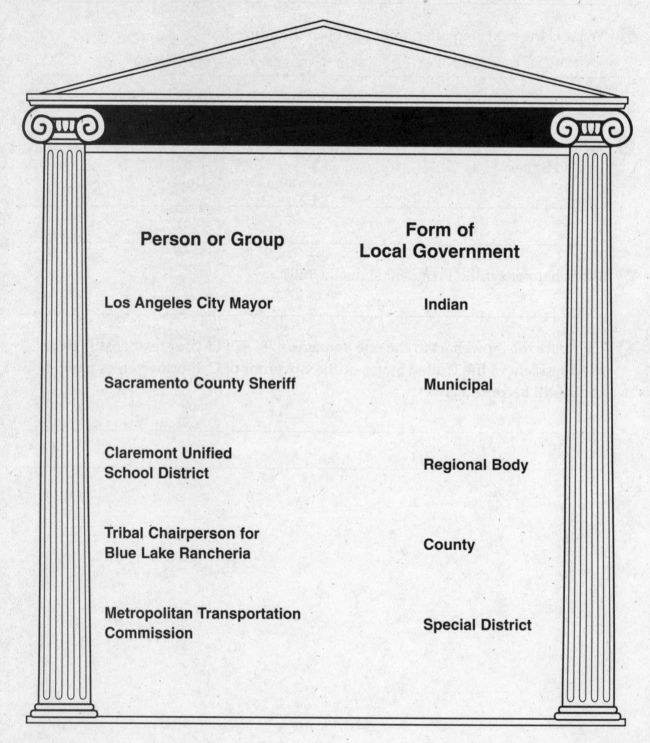

Person or Group	Form of Local Government
Los Angeles City Mayor	Indian
Sacramento County Sheriff	Municipal
Claremont Unified School District	Regional Body
Tribal Chairperson for Blue Lake Rancheria	County
Metropolitan Transportation Commission	Special District

CALIFORNIA STANDARDS HSS 4.5, 4.5.5

(continued)

© Harcourt

Use after reading Chapter 12, Lesson 3, pages 480–487.

Name _____ Date _____

DIRECTIONS Answer the questions below about local governments.

1 What is a regional body?

_____

_____

2 A county board of supervisors does the work of which branch or branches of the government?

_____

_____

3 What is the difference between general law cities and charter cities?

_____

_____

4 List three ways that a sovereign Indian tribe is like its own nation.

_____

_____

_____

5 Why is it important for the office of education for each county to work with the state board of education and local school districts?

_____

_____

Name _____ Date _____

Skills: Make an Economic Decision

DIRECTIONS Imagine you are the mayor of Anytown, California. The city council has just approved the budget for next year. You have $10,000 to spend on "extras" for the town. You feel that Anytown needs police and fire department upgrades, roadwork on Main Street, new playground equipment for the park, school maintenance equipment, and new chairs for the library. You would also like to have an Independence Day parade and a Harvest Festival.

Look at the list of costs below. Choose how to spend the "extras" budget for Anytown, and answer the questions.

Anytown "Extras" Budget	$10,000.00
Police department upgrade	$2,500.00
Fire department upgrade	$2,500.00
Roadwork on Main Street	$1,500.00
New playground equipment	$1,500.00
School maintenance equipment	$3,000.00
New chairs for Anytown Library	$2,000.00
Independence Day parade	$500.00
Harvest Festival	$1,000.00

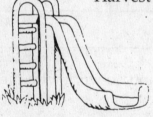

1 What do you think are the three most important budget items to spend money on? Explain your answer.

_____

_____

_____

_____

_____

CALIFORNIA STANDARDS HSS 4.5, 4.5.4; HI 4

(continued)

134 ▪ Homework and Practice Book   Use after reading Chapter 12, Skill Lesson, pages 488–489.

© Harcourt

Name _____ Date _____

2 Based on the budget, how would you spend the $10,000.00? Remember that the budget cannot add up to more than $10,000.00.

_____

_____

_____

_____

_____

3 Suppose you must choose between doing roadwork on Main Street and buying new playground equipment. Choosing one of these things means that you are giving up the other. What is it called when you give up one thing to get something else?

_____

4 What were the opportunity costs of your budget?

_____

_____

5 Did you decide to have an Independence Day parade or a Harvest Festival in your budget? Why or why not? Why are social events important to the town?

_____

_____

_____

_____

Chapter 12

Name _____ Date _____

Study Guide

DIRECTIONS Todd wrote an article for his school newspaper about the governments of the United States and California. Fill in the missing words or phrases in Todd's article. Use the terms below to help you.

Lesson 1	Lesson 2	Lesson 3
federal	bill	municipal
democracy	budget	special districts
amendments	veto	board of supervisors
Congress	recall	jury trials
taxes	referendum	sovereign

Lesson 1   Government plays an important role in our lives. This article will explain about the governments of the United States and California. The United States has a form of government known as a

_____, in which the people rule by making decisions themselves or by electing people to make decisions for them. The

_____ government is located in Washington, D.C. It includes the Senate and the House of Representatives, which make up

_____. The United States Constitution is kept up to date

through changes, or _____. All levels of government

collect _____, or money from citizens to help pay

for services.

CALIFORNIA STANDARDS HSS 4.5, 4.5.1, 4.5.3, 4.5.4, 4.5.5   (continued)

136 ■ Homework and Practice Book   Use after reading Chapter 12, pages 462–491.

Name _____ Date _____

Lesson 2 The California State Legislature is similar to the United States

Congress. It has two houses, called the senate and the assembly. Members of

each house can present a plan for a new law, or a _____.

After each house approves a new law, it goes to the governor. If the governor

does not agree with it, he or she can _____ the law.

The legislature then needs two-thirds of its members to approve the law

for it to pass. California's governor is responsible for enforcing the state's

laws. The governor is also responsible for creating a plan for how to spend

state money, called a _____. Voters in California

can take action against a law by asking that citizens vote on it through a

_____. California voters can remove elected officials

from office through a _____.

Lesson 3 California's highest level of local government is the county

government. The county's voters elect a group of leaders called the

_____. Each county has a judicial branch and a

superior court. These courts may hear _____, or

cases in which citizens decide if the person is guilty or not guilty. City,

or _____, governments pass local laws and see that

these laws are obeyed. _____ sometimes provide

services that county or city governments do not provide. Indian tribes

have their own governments. The tribes can form free and independent, or

_____, governments on their lands.

© Harcourt

Name _____ Date _____

READING SOCIAL STUDIES: SUMMARIZE

 Californians and Government

DIRECTIONS Complete the graphic organizers to show that you understand how to summarize about Californians and the government.

Key Fact

All levels of government operate only with citizens' approval.

Summary

_____

_____

_____

_____

_____

_____

_____

_____

Key Fact

Each level of government can only exist with written laws that are accepted by the people.

Key Fact

In the California Constitution, voters have the power to pass initiatives.

Summary

_____

_____

_____

_____

_____

_____

_____

_____

Key Fact

In California, voters can recall state officials.

© Harcourt

CALIFORNIA STANDARDS HSS 4.5, 4.5.2, 4.5.3